BLEWBURY "In one year and out the other"

Edited by Ron Freeborn and Robert Long
Published By The Blewbury Village Society 2010
Copyright © Ron Freeborn

ISBN: 978-0-9553992-1-3

Photographers and artists are attributed alongside pictures, either explicitly or using initials as follows:
BM: Bernard Mattimore   DS: Dick Street   EL-J: Elphin Lloyd-Jones   JD: June Downey
PW: Peter Willison   RF: Ron Freeborn   RL: Robert Long   SJ: Sally Jones

Views expressed In the book are those of the individual authors of articles.

The moral right of the contributors has been asserted. All rights reserved.

Printed by Technique Studios, Banbury

FOREWORD

What Blewbury is

Blewbury is a medium sized village in Oxfordshire, with a population in 2009 of about 1600 people. It was, until some 50 years ago, a typical agricultural village many centuries old (then in the county of Berkshire), even though it had a surprising number of writers and artists who had escaped here from London. It is well endowed with attractive old houses and footpaths as well as an ancient church. Over recent decades it has changed a great deal however. Many of its inhabitants now owe their living, directly or indirectly, to the various scientific research establishments nearby (the Harwell 'Atomic', for example, as it was often known locally). Others live here because of the easy travel (fast trains and fast roads) which allows them to commute to work in Oxford, Reading and London.

The village, like many other villages, has always put on local fêtes, plays, musical events and sporting events, but in recent years the scope of these has increased a great deal. Hence this book.

This Book

The book records a year in the village – the calendar year 2009 – as an informal diary of the local events which are characteristic of Blewbury. It is designed as a 'Time Capsule' aimed at people fifty years ahead in 2059, whom we hope will find it curious and – hopefully – interesting. Chris Lakeland has given the book its subtitle "in one year and out the other" which says it all.

We have tried to give a flavour of all sorts of aspects of Blewbury life, including mundane features of everyday lives – buses, postal deliveries, shopping lists and the like – as well as the major village events – the opera, the festival, Twelfth Night, the Boxing Day walk and so on. To put the life of the village into a wider context we decided to include short reminders of some of the national or international events that happened in 2009. We are very grateful to Doreen Laugharne who went through copies of the *Times* all through the year noting these, as well as to June Downey who kept a diary month by month of international, national and local events.

We also circulated a questionnaire around the village asking people for their various comments about what life here is like. The answers have often been unexpected and amusing, and we have included quotations from these here and there throughout the book.

At the back you will see a map of the village which shows places to which the articles refer, and you will also see grateful acknowledgments to all those people who have put a huge amount of work into putting the book together.

The book has been sponsored by the Blewbury Village Society, which is an umbrella organisation designed to support and encourage a wide variety of village activities, to which all residents automatically belong. We are very grateful for this support.

Robert Long, Blewbury, June 2010

JANUARY

Zak Corderoy - photo Tim Corderoy

Jan 23 A concert at Richard Blackford's house raised £1525 for the Stepping Stones Orphanage in India   - BM

British Junior 8.5 production Mini Moto Champion 2009

Zak Corderoy, aged 10, competed in two championships in 2009.

In the British Championship, consisting of 9 rounds all over the UK, Zak came first on his production bike.

He was also champion in the NPS (National Pocketbike Series), riding his production bike.

Tim Corderoy

 **LOCAL NEWS**

Jan 11 The ultimate recycling? Seen in Westbrook Street – a man cycling towards Savages with a Christmas tree for recycling, tied to the bike, being dragged along the road.

Jan 14 *Didcot Herald:* The bay mare Belle Fleur, owned by Jane Dexter of Blewbury Riding Stables, has qualified for the British Open Show Jumping Championships in Birmingham in April.

Jan 16 The local MP, Ed Vaizey, presents an Eco award to Blewbury School *(Didcot Herald).*

Jan 20 Tea and crumpets followed by champagne at Richard & Norma Bird's house, watching the TV reporting and celebrating Barack Obama's inauguration as President of the USA.

JANUARY

MARMALADE January is the month when Savages sell Seville Oranges which make the best marmalade. Here are two recipes.

3lb (1.5kg) oranges Juice of 2 lemons 6lb (3kg) sugar 4 pints (2litres) water Makes about 10lb (5kg)

Put the oranges and lemon juice in a large pan. Cover with 4 pints water. Bring the pan to the boil, cover. Place in low oven for few hours (bottom oven of an Aga is ideal) to make fruit easy to cut up.

Next lift out the fruit. Leave the orange liquid in the pan. Cut oranges in half. Scoop out all the pips and pith and add these to the liquid in the pan. Bring to the boil for 6 minutes with lid off. Strain this liquid through a sieve, pressing the pulp through with a wooden spoon. Pour this liquid into a large pan.

Cut up the peel as thin as you like it. Add it to the liquid in the pan with the sugar. Stir until sugar has dissolved. Then boil rapidly 15-20 minutes until setting point is reached (tested by placing a drop or two onto a cold plate and see if it shows first signs of wrinkling). Leave in pan for 10 minutes to cool a little then pot, seal and label.

Kathy Edmunds

2lb oranges   2 lemons 9lb Sugar   7 pints water

Recipe as supplied to me:

Remove pips, squeeze and mince fruit. Cover pips with some water (in a little bowl). Steep pulp in remaining water for 24-48 hrs. Put pips in bag and boil and simmer until peel is soft. Add sugar, dissolve and boil to gel. Leave in pan for a few minutes then put in jars.

My version:

This makes a light jellyish marmalade but can take a long time to reach setting point.

Boil whole fruit in pressure cooker for 6 minutes with a small amount of water. Cool. Scrape inside from fruit and put into a muslin bag. Mince all skins. Boil to setting point with minced fruit, bagged pith etc. and ONLY about 6 pints water in total.

Mary Marshall

Jan 1 Roger Cambray Memorial Walk - *Bulletin February*

Another record gathering! 50 people and assorted dogs walked this year. We also had two ladies from Didcot who had seen the notice in the Herald and decided to join us. It was one of the most beautiful January 1sts we've had for the walk - blue sky, bright sun and no wind. The frost of the preceding few days made the walking firm and mainly dry. Many thanks again to all who came and to those who drove there to carry back those unhappy about walking back as well. See you next year (and see the back cover).

The Blackies

NATIONAL AND OVERSEAS EVENTS

Jan 1 Happy 150th Birthday to Big Ben – the famous bell in the Clock Tower in Westminster.

Jan 2 Slowing coral growth may spell disaster for Great Barrier Reef *(Times)*.

Jan 5 Israel's rain of fire on Gaza – phosphorus shells screen ground assault *(Times)*.

Jan 14 1013 Gaza citizens reportedly killed by Israeli forces since the beginning of the war on 27 December 2008. 13 Israeli losses.

Jan 16 All 150 passengers survive when a US Airways Airbus plane has to make an emergency crash landing in the Hudson River, New York *(Times)*.

Jan 20 Barack Hussein Obama inaugurated as the first black President of the USA.

Jan 31 Strikes at 19 UK sites over 'British jobs for British workers' *(Times)*.

JANUARY
Keeping Blewbury going

Volunteer litter remover Jane Gibson - BM

Hazel, Kevin and Mark —the recycling team - JD

Mobile library - BM

Mark Street– third generation coalman - BM

JANUARY
Keeping Blewbury going

Jerry the postman delivering in Grahame Close   -   JD

Ian the Milkman   -   JD

Kim the fish man   -   BM

JANUARY

Blewbury's cob walls

Right: From Red Lion towards Play Close - BM

Below right: Curtoys Lane - BM

Spring - SJ

JANUARY

Blewbury's cob walls

From Methodist Chapel to Church Road - BM

From Play Close towards Red Lion   Photo Paul Whitehead

Wall built in 1995 - PW

COB WALLS Blewbury has more thatched cob walls than any other village in England. The six intriguing structures are a unique feature of the village. They are thought to be Saxon in origin and are listed buildings. Five of the walls are privately owned and maintained. The sixth wall, in Curtoys Lane (near the centre of the village), is looked after by The Cob Wall committee, which raises funds to repair and maintain it. The cost of re-thatching is considerable at about £100 per metre, and is required about every fifteen years so there is a need to raise money every year in readiness. In 2009 the Council for the Rural Protection of England donated £500 and the wall is currently in a good state of repair. A short section of new cob wall, next to the Red Lion, was added by volunteers using traditional methods in 1995.

The walls are built on a low plinth of assorted flint, chalk and bricks. The cob itself is made of marl, the local subsoil layer consisting of decayed matter and clay-like chalk. It is built up layer by layer, perhaps six inches at a time, and allowed to dry out somewhat before the next layer is added. Straw is mixed in if the marl is very wet. It has been freely used in local buildings for thousands of years.   The thatch must be kept in good condition or the soft cob is quickly eroded by rain and frost. It is therefore quite remarkable that these structures have survived for centuries even after knowledge of their original purpose has been lost in the mists of time. The village is very proud of them and 2009 saw some minor repairs and much interest from the community and visitors alike.   *Paul Whitehead*

FEBRUARY

Snowman - *RL*

See 'All ready to go!' in Local Events below left - BM

LOCAL EVENTS

Feb 1 Snow one inch deep. More fell later in the week – 5 inches deep on 5 Feb.

Feb 8 All ready to go! – Richard Blackford, Jo Laugharne and lots of volunteer animals at the initial gathering for the opera *Noyes Fludde* (photo above right).

During February: The Parish Council donated £300 to the fund for the Curtoys Lane cob wall. Peter Cockrell filled some holes in the same wall. Bob and Amanda at the Red Lion got the cob wall section near the Red Lion rethatched (paid for by Brakspears). It looks really great.

NATIONAL AND OVERSEAS EVENTS

Feb 9 The worst ever bush fires in Australia raged for several days, claiming at least 170 lives and leaving 1500 homeless.

Feb 12 Morgan Tsvangirai given a euphoric welcome as Prime Minister in Zimbabwe. Robert Mugabe remains as President (*Times*).

Feb 17 Dee Caffari (she's British) becomes the first woman to sail around the globe solo in both directions (*Times*).

Feb 24 British resident Binyam Mohamed released from US prison at Guantánamo Bay after seven years detention without charge.

Feb 26 Up to 60,000 bank workers worldwide face losing jobs as the Royal Bank of Scotland and Lloyds Bank prepare to wield the axe.

FEBRUARY

First orchestral rehearsal for the Noyes Fludde opera, in the Methodist Chapel - RF

Blewbury Methodist Church 2009 – the end or a rebirth?

We have been here by the Cleve since 1826, so a fair bit has happened to us before now, but 2009 was a significant year for us – our building was used by more people in 2009 than ever before, but the end of the year was the end of our church as we know it!

The church is looking good – we have a new floor, new windows and are newly decorated. And the community is using our building for so many different things, not just meetings, coffee mornings and the monthly Foot Clinic. It was used for 12th Night rehearsals when it rained, and the *Noye's Fludde* musicians played together for the first time as an orchestra here. The BVS showed films and held their Winter Lecture Series and we hosted six Festival events. The Bridge Club are teaching learners here, the Parish Council use the church for some of their meetings (I hear people are more restrained in what they say at the meetings in church). In fact the only use we have refused this year was Egyptian Dancing classes!

In 2009 we also faced a big decision about how we could ensure there will continue to be a Methodist Church in Blewbury in years to come. Our members voted in October 2009 to combine with the Upton Methodists to become the new Spring Line Methodist Church - one church with two Centres, in Blewbury and in Upton. Why Spring Line? Both buildings lie on the spring line that links Upton and Blewbury, the line of springs that are the reason the villages evolved where they are.

The new Spring Line Church was born on January 1st 2010. Do come to visit us, not only on week days but on Sundays as well.

Jo Lakeland, and the members of the Spring Line Methodist Church

FEBRUARY

The Church in Blewbury

A Year in the Life of St. Michael's Church.

St. Michael's is an open church, open all day, every day and through these open doors have come people of all ages for all manner of reasons. The bedrock of this church is the Christian faith expressed in varying forms; the glorious sung Eucharist led by the choir, with the Sunday School quietly joining at the Communion, before showing us, with great enthusiasm, what they have been creating in the Benefice Centre; and much more. The church is open for quiet prayer, for silent vigil, when the ancient, stone walls exclude the noisy world and there is peace.

Blewbury is in the care of our resident Rector, Revd Jason St. John Nicolle who looks after six parishes, helped by Revd Louise Butler and Revd Anthony Lury.

We are summoned by the ringing of the eight ancient bells to this significant presence in the centre of the village with its huge capacity for large gatherings. 2009 has seen:

- Children dressed as animals have marched in two by two to the music of Benjamin Britten's *Noyes Fludde* to join a huge cast and participating audience in this community opera. The Nave was transformed into the Ark.
- *Music for a Summer's Evening* during the Festival and the Art Exhibition which filled the interior for three days before the Festival Finale's celebration of local talent.
- The Oxford Concerto Orchestra entertaining us on a warm July evening.
- The Family Service in August on the Playclose, a perfect location.
- The sound of tea cups, conversation and laughter wafted out from Teas in Church on Sundays.
- Young members at a weekly bible study and discussion group.
- Dark November bringing the sombre service of Remembrance for all the fallen from the First World War to the current conflict in Afghanistan.
- A week later an amusing, skilful rendition of the words and music of Joyce Grenfell.
- Shining white lights on the pine tree hauled onto the Church tower heralding Christmas.
- Sunday School's colourful performance of the Nativity play.
- Snowy boots banged against the walls before people packed inside for the ever popular Carol Concert, with the impromptu orchestra and the rousing, uninhibited singing of favourite carols.
- The Crib Service on Christmas Eve, and Midnight Mass, tiny candles lodged on every ledge, in every nook and cranny, magically lighting the interior for this enduring service. Two more services on Christmas Day.

All the year round through these open doors have passed the Ministry Team, Baptism Visitors, Marriage Preparation Organizers, Bereavement Visitors, the Mothers' Union supporting the monthly Pram Service and those helping at Youth Club.

On the final Sunday of the year the faithful gathered together to observe their commitment to the Christian faith and to maintain this open church for all people.

Isobel Street

The Church in Blewbury   FEBRUARY

Church altar - DS

Below left: Spring - BM

Path on east side of churchyard - SJ

FEBRUARY

David Harber designs and makes a spectacular range of sundials and garden sculptures. He donated a sundial to raise money for the Blewbury Open Gardens in 2009 (photos David Harber).

FEBRUARY

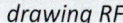
drawing RF

Orchard Dene Barn

This barn has been used by the Blewbury Players for many years, for scenery construction and storage as well as for dressing and makeup for the Players' Theatre in the garden of Orchard Dene. It is now being converted into a private house under the name of Watt's Barn, while the Players have a substantial new storeroom behind for their continuing use of the theatre. The photo on the right (BM) shows the moving out ceremony in January 2009. Rebuilding the barn has been a major exercise involving a lot of new roof timbers, as will be obvious from the photo above (PW).

13

MARCH

drawing RF

Pancake Race outside the Charity School - BM

LOCAL EVENTS

Mar 7   Blewbury's challenge for top spot in North Berks Football League Division 1 suffered a blow (*Didcot Herald*).
Mar 15   First spring-like day of the year. Temperatures up to 15C.
During March, the Village Hall once again suffered from smashed windows. Impact marks on the surviving windows suggested that the damage was caused largely by footballs.
Mar 31 The March Winter Lecture was quite different to anything seen before — see the article on Winter Lectures

MARCH

BLEWBURY'S BAND

Blewbury Brass Band has spent some of its energy, in 2009, planning what we should do in 2010 when we will be celebrating our centenary (the band's, not us personally). The Band was formed in October 1910 by a committee of local worthies, with the stated aim of 'keeping the youngsters off the streets'. It has continued playing ever since, apart from breaks during the two world wars when many of the players were in the forces. Not many village brass bands can claim that.

So what might we do? We had a singalong in the Playclose in 2005 (as a money-raising venture for Ladycroft Park's legal expenses) and it looks as if that is a popular idea for next year. We have already recruited another musical group or two to take turns playing with the band – you can't play a brass instrument for more than 40 minutes without your lips going all wobbly – and we are planning a pig roast. To mark the year Steve Russell and Julian Gallop have been hard at work preparing a history of the band. We are all looking forward to our 100th birthday.

Jag Cook, Band President and Secretary - SJ

2009 has been a busy year. Under our musical director, Bob Knight, we have played twice at Newbury Bandstand, at fêtes in Oxfordshire as well as in foreign parts (Berkshire). We played with Didcot Choral Society in East Hagbourne Church (in aid of their Organ Fund). We opened the Blewbury Festival with an opening fanfare at the Family Fun Day, and closed it at the Festival Evensong. Under Alex's supervision, several of our members formed the cornet section for *Noyes' Fludde*. As usual, our regular autumn/winter fixtures included the Remembrance Service, the Christmas concert in the church, and, of course, playing for carol singing on the Play Close during Father Christmas's visit to Blewbury. Christmas also brings carol playing for charity in Didcot and Newbury. Band numbers are larger than they have been for many years – and we have been especially pleased to welcome some of the members of Claire Eisenhandler's learners' band into the main band this year.

Blewbury Band may not be quite in the Black Dyke Mills class (we're working on it) but we do enjoy ourselves!

Robert Long

The Band at the bandstand in Victoria Park, Newbury in September 2009 (photo James Howlett)

MARCH

The Diary of a Gossip Aged 59½

Diary Entry

Dress Rehearsal - Noye's Fludde

Dress rehearsal went quite well. Nobody lost their temper (well not really). We all seemed to leave intact and I think it will be a good show. What an abundance of musical talent we have unearthed and unleashed. It would be a great pity if we lose energy in this. How could we keep the momentum going? What could we do next? How do we keep up the interest and enthusiasm? What about another Opera or a Show?

Sir Gawain and the Green Knight, a brilliant experience in 1978. Lots of kids involved in that - they were really good - but all in parts and pretty tricky. Memo to self – must talk to........

What about developing singing skills for another opera - singing workshops? We had some years ago. Olga ran them. Potential opera participants felt much more confident and several auditioned. Memo to self – must talk to....

Think back to 1985 *Blewbury a Song for Europe*, a complete spoof of the Eurovision Song Contest but with a really good quality of original music and musicianship. This was a really successful Blewbury show, but 20 years ago and with very little technology....could work. Wouldn't it be good to do this again with modern technology. Memo to self – must talk to...

...That's the problem with this village...somebody has an idea...then people start talking, and before you know it...

> Future Events definitely planned:
> Singing Workshops scheduled for February 2010
> *Blewbury - A Song for Europe* scheduled for May 2011
> *Sir Gawain and the Green Knight* scheduled for Autumn 2011/Spring 2012

Anon.

Questionnaire Answers

Tell us your favourite part of the village.

Grahame Close — and I like very much the track, the field and the stream that start behind the school and post office …..
Our favourite part is Grahame Close too. Although there are no roads to cross, you still have to cross 3 bridges over the stream to reach the pub! It always makes it fun on the way back when it's dark…..
Watts Lane going towards the Church…….Dibleys…The streams and paths…..Nottingham Fee…..
Hard one! The play close down beside the stream…..
The view across the Cochrane's meadow from Watery Lane...

NATIONAL AND OVERSEAS EVENTS

Mar 3 Terrorists attacked the Sri Lankan cricket team in Lahore. Several police killed and cricketers also injured, though not seriously.

Mar 5 UK Bank interest rate reduced to lowest ever of 0.5%

Mar 11 Unemployment figures in the UK have reached nearly 2 million.

Mar 16 The Chief Medical Officer remarked that Britain has a drinking problem and suggested putting up the prices of alcohol to at least 50p per unit. The Government ruled out his proposal.

Mar 20 Sean Hodgson freed from prison after serving 27 years. DNA has now proved that he could not have been the murderer.

Mar 27 Parliament is to debate allowing an heir to the throne to marry a Roman Catholic and for the line of succession to be allowed to appoint a female ahead of her younger male siblings.

Mar 31 US President Obama arrived in the UK with his wife for his first visit since taking office.

ASHBROOK GARDENS

A private garden, but one used to host events for the village and beyond for as long as can be remembered, 2009 saw the usual welcome visitors and some not so welcome!

The year started with an out of the blue 'phone call from the Natural History Museum - was it genuine? After a degree of scepticism, genuine it was. A particularly rare organism had been found in the Millbrook lower down in the village, and the Museum's botanists wanted to know whether its discovery was isolated or whether it was to be found elsewhere in the stream - where better to look than in Ashbrook where the stream rises? (Shouldn't it therefore be called the Ashbrook?). Sure enough, it was found, but there the excitement ends - it is too small and indistinct to be recognisable.

March saw the first of the two annual open days under the auspices of the National Garden Scheme. The garden has been opening for more than 50 years now, and by us for 25 years - five years ago we were presented with a silver trowel, an honour for owners whose gardens have opened for 20 years. The second opening was in early September and there was a real contrast in the garden between the bareness in March, allowing the spring bulbs to show off to their full glory, and the colour and density of the vegetation in September. The NGS supports many charities, particularly the Macmillan Nurses specialising in cancer care – our favourite charity.

Between the two NGS openings, the garden hosted the Village Festival's summer dance. The weather held out (just) and 250 revellers had a wonderful evening picnicking, barbecuing and dancing on the lawns. No village festival goes by without the Ashbrook (sorry, Millbrook) Walk, which starts in the garden and traces through private gardens until it reaches the Mill - this has been a highlight of the festival for many years.

Visitors are not limited to the human variety - the lake has been restocked this year with trout, and that has attracted the heron — at the same time a welcome and unwelcome visitor. All three varieties of woodpecker were seen in the garden, as was the kingfisher and, of course, the red kite. A grass snake put in an appearance, as did the muntjac deer and rabbits (neither of the latter two particularly welcomed by the gardener). Notable absentees were the fox (the chickens asked for that to be noted), and the parish councillors (but that is another story).

Simon Barrett

MARCH

Ashbrook Gardens
Photos Jane Barrett

MARCH Food Cupboard

AND WHAT DID THE ITEMS IN THIS CUPBOARD COST?
(prices recorded at Sainsbury's Didcot)

ITEM	£	ITEM	£
Cheerios	2.30	John West Tuna Steak	1.55
Merlot	8.59	Sharwood Mango Chutney	1.75
Ambrosia Custard	1.49	Chopped Tomatoes	0.59
Raspberry Jelly	0.39	Hellmann's Mayonnaise	2.82
Marmite	2.25	Bournville Cocoa	2.20
Homepride Flour	0.93	Runny Honey	2.20
Vegetable Oil	0.99	Nescafé Espresso Coffee	3.29
Lasagne Sheets	0.60	Water Chestnuts	2.99
Cadbury Chocolate Tin	2.99	Tomato Ketchup	2.63
Sage & Onion Stuffing	1.18	Spam	1.82
Uncle Ben's Rice	4.83	Anchovies	0.74
Colman's Tartare Sauce	0.90	Heinz Beans	0.51

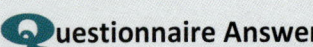

Questionnaire Answers

What does £10 buy you?

Mobile Top Up at the post office.

A car wash and clean

A child's hair cut at the hairdressers

Loads of sweets

A week's worth of vegetables in Savages

2.5 bales of hay

38 eggs from Ange

A disco ticket

2 glasses of wine, with a bit of change if small glasses

5/6s of a taxi to Tesco

Just over 17 pints of milk from the milkman (58p each)

Fuel for about 90 miles in the car (but no petrol or diesel is sold in Blewbury)

14 days' supply of newspapers

photo BM

MARCH

Left: Rory Young carving an armorial cartouche at a house in Wiltshire

Right: His carving of Noah (Noye in Blewbury spelling) building the Ark, at the Great West Door of York Minster

Photos Rory Young

Marianne Suhr is a Historic Buildings Surveyor and is a co-presenter of the BBC's 'Restoration' programme.

Winter Lectures

Winter evenings are so dull, so it seemed a good idea to liven them up a bit with a series of evening talks. I started the Blewbury Winter Lectures in January 2009. My contacts were limited to old building specialists, but that seemed a fitting topic for Blewbury given all the wibbly wobbly houses in this village.

James Ayres, Author of 'Vernacular Interiors, the British Tradition' started things off by talking about the evolution of the humble cottage including wall decoration, floor coverings, fireplaces and much more.

Rory Young, artist, craftsman and expert in historic building repair followed in February, giving an illustrated talk about the works to his own townhouse in Cirencester. Through his eye for detail and love of design he created a stunningly beautiful home.

Charles Brooking has been rescuing windows, doors, and other period fittings out of roadside skips since the age of three (yes, three). Now, with over 10,000 items in his collection (he has an impressive collection of barns and sheds, too, to hold them), he is one of the leading authorities on the construction and dating of traditional joinery. This was an interactive session, with examples from Charles' collection as well as bits from Blewbury houses.

And I finished the season off in April by describing a previous project of mine – the rescue of a 300 year old 'little Brick House'.

This winter I thought we might diversify a little, so we've kicked off with a December lecture on chairs. Proud owners struggled through the icy winter chill to bring along their most prized possessions and Bill Cotton, the authority on the subject, amazed us with his knowledge of each one. The Methodist Chapel has been a cosy and comfortable venue for the talks, and all proceeds will go towards its upkeep.

Marianne Suhr

APRIL

Noye's Fludde

Opera finale in Blewbury church - PW

A Son's point of View

I can still remember sitting in Richard's lovely house, waiting nervously for our audition to begin. There were lots of girls, lots of nervous laughter, a gorgeous grand piano and the wonderful parts of Noah's sons and wives up for grabs!

Here I am now, nearly one year and countless laughs later, telling the story of my part in *Noye's Fludde*. Seven of us were lucky enough to play one of these wonderful roles, Immy, Freya, Grace, Rosie, Zoe, Chloe and me, Eloise. We didn't really know each other all that well at the beginning but one of the best things we got out of the opera was friendship and a shared experience. We are all still in touch.

Taking part in *Noye's Fludde* was like being part of a huge, if slightly dysfunctional family. At times I wondered if we would ever perfect the lines and music cues whilst animals of every shape and colour wandered on and off stage either on or slightly off cue! Despite all our concerns, the crazy and chaotic rehearsals, we worked really hard and in the end we did it and the performances were a huge success.

We worked with a team of brilliant people including, Jo Laugharne director, Richard Blackford musical director and Ron Freeborn designer and so many more. All of these people worked tirelessly to make the opera a huge success and they pulled it off. Who would have thought a small community could create and perfect an opera written by no less than Benjamin Britten?

Sixty four animals, Noah's family, a bunch of drunk gossips and a huge orchestra later and we were ready to perform. Standing outside in the freezing cold, waiting to run in cheerily and sing our parts, nerves began to take over. What if we forgot the words, or couldn't reach that tricky note? But I didn't, and neither did anyone else and the audience loved it. I still remember the sense of achievement and as we processed outside with ringing of applause in our ears, it was without doubt one of the best moments of my life. Being part of *Noye's Fludde* gave me and the other girls a real sense of community, of belonging to Blewbury, that will stay with us for the rest of our lives. It was a huge privilege and great fun to be part of it.

Eloise Carey, aged 12

APRIL

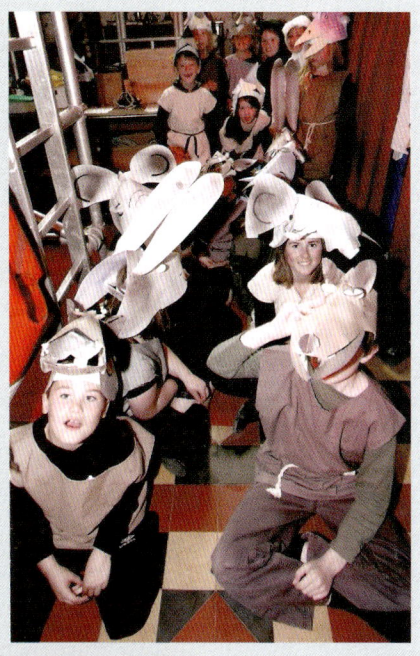

Noah's animals (top left photo Chris Willison), and behind the scenes (top right BM)

Noah and Mrs. Noah (lower far left BM)

The gossips (lower centre BM)

APRIL   *Easter*

Blewbury chalk pit — photo Graham Richards

Egg Rolling at the Chalk Pit
I was organising the egg rolling this year. I took the loudhailer and Easter egg prizes up in a wheelbarrow together with a broom to sweep the track and pegs to mark the winning distances. I would say there were about 60 people and two dogs who rolled their eggs. Many traditionalists started their egg rolling using their noses. This technique I think was started by Hugh Pickles and it did seem to increase the distance the egg rolled. Many adults who were Blewbury children were back to visit family and after the event stayed on the downs to chat and catch up.   *Graham Richards*

The Duck Race
St Michael's bellringers held a Duck Race on Easter Sunday, 4th April, in the Playclose. The first of five heats started at 12.00 noon. The first three ducks across the line in the final race won £50, £20 and £10 respectively, and all proceeds went to St Michael's Tower and Bell Maintenance Fund. We are very appreciative of the support given by the village to this annual event, and hope that everyone enjoyed the fun.

This event was open to everyone, and racing ducks were available for £1 (yes, these ducks are inflation proof!).

Due to the popularity of this event, racing Ducks are always sold out before the day, so it is always important for villagers to contact the bellringers early to avoid disappointment. Everyone was asked not to forget to come along, and to bring their family and friends to cheer for the ducks on the day.   *Richard Loyd*

photo JD

NATIONAL AND OVERSEAS EVENTS
Apr 1 President Obama and Michelle Obama met the Queen.

Apr 3 Wisden Cricketer's Almanack honours Clare Taylor as first ever woman to be nominated Cricketer of the Year (*Times*).

Apr 16 The Transport Secretary announced incentives of up to £5,000 for consumers to buy electric cars.

Apr 22 Budget Day. In South Africa the African National Party re-elected, led by Jacob Zuma.

Apr 29 Carol Ann Duffy offered the post of Poet Laureate – the first woman to be so honoured (*Times*).

Apr 30 4,000 British troops stationed in Basra leaving Iraq after handing over control to the USA. 179 British servicemen and women have died there since the invasion of Iraq in March 2003.

*Red Lion
quiz night
RF*

APRIL

 **LOCAL EVENTS**

Apr 1   Blewbury Primary School triumphed in the Vale of White Horse Under 11 girls' six-a-side football tournament.

Apr 12   (Easter Sunday) St Michael's Bellringers held a Duck Race for 500 plastic ducks in the Playclose (proceeds to St Michael's Tower and Bell Maintenance Fund). The Village Society ran the Egg Rolling Competition at The Chalk Pit.

Apr 22 to 25 *Noyes Fludde* performed at St. Michael's Church.

Apr 25 500 photograph taken in churchyard.

Apr 29 Quiz night with bangers and mash at the Red Lion.

New Local History Group website www.blewburyhistory.org.uk .

Peregrine falcon and little white egret seen in Blewbury.

Questionnaire Answers

An Ideal Day

Catless…..Walking over Blewburton for lunch at The Sweet Olive…..

Sledging on Blewburton….Playing in the stream at the Red Lion all day…..

Cycling to the Playgroup for work then meeting a friend at the Red Lion for lunch. In the evening playing Badminton in the Village Hall…..Saturday or Sunday...

What National/International event mattered to you

I should say some great disaster or Obama - but I will remember it as being the "Credit Crunch hits home" year…..The deaths of so many young men in Afghanistan…..The increasing/ongoing threat of climate change and its impact on our children's future…..The iron man competition. Since I saw the documentary about it I'm training to do it next year!.....Obama winning USA election...

Tell us a secret

It isn't the slugs that eat my beans - it's the dratted rabbit!.....There is an early morning litter picker - an unsung heroine…..

Somewhere in the village are the lost graves of the Quakers…..Barbra Streisand once used the toilet in the Petrol Station...

APRIL

Blewbury residents were photographed from the top of the Church tower in the shapes of the digits 5, 0 and 0.

The crowd in place waiting for the middle '0' photo to be taken - RL

What happened on April 25th?

That was the day a lot of Blewbury residents turned up at the churchyard for the '500 photo' used for the cover of Bulletin issue 500. For space reasons in the churchyard, the digits had to be photographed separately and combined later by electronic wizardry.

We were curious and a bit apprehensive to know how many people would actually come. We needed about 350 to form the shapes of 5, 0 and 0, without anyone appearing more than once. In fact the number of people on the Bulletin 500 cover is 382, not forgetting at least two dogs. So there was no difficulty. That includes everyone who came, and mystery extras such as Bernard Mattimore, who actually took the photos, Dick Street who masterminded the operations at the top of the tower, and Isobel Street who guarded the *Noye's Fludde* stage set inside the church.

The Bulletin is very grateful to them all and particularly grateful to Elphin Lloyd-Jones, who used the latest computer techniques to replace the white template cloth with grass, going carefully around the shape of everyone in the picture. He then moved a few people who were standing outside the template, added those who were missing for various reasons and joined the three photos together, leaving out the tombstones. The job took at least 60 hours of his time.

And we are very grateful to everyone who came and smiled up at Bernard to make what is a memorable souvenir.

The Bulletin Team

APRIL

The actual photo taken of the digit '5' - BM

Two advisers helping Elphin decide where people are to stand - RL

Bottom left: A thank you cake for the volunteers who help with the Bulletin - RL

Below: the final result - BM

MAY

Thermal image of Spring Cottage taken by the Environment Group revealing hidden beams behind stucco facing, which the owners were unaware of. Lower central window is double glazed — the others are not! (surface temperature scale from 6.2 to 14.3 C).

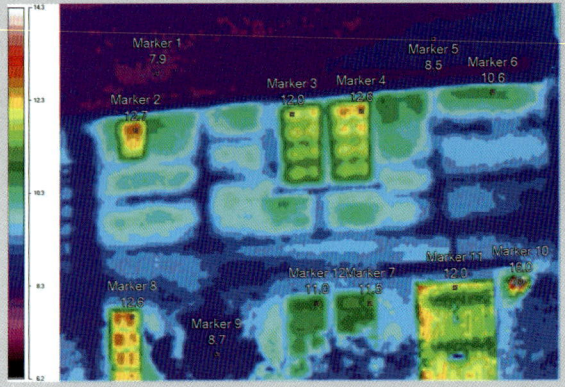

Energy Initiative Survey Results
(Bulletin issue 499)

Over the last two months or so we have been surveying the actions people in Blewbury have taken to save energy over the last 3 years. This was partly to guide the discussion on the future of the Energy Initiative. We asked a sample of the households in Blewbury to complete a questionnaire and received 112 replies. Thanks to everyone who replied. 96% of replies stated that the household has taken some action to reduce energy consumption.

The strongest pressures were probably the increased cost of fuel and the government drive to introduce low energy lighting. It seems that 90% of households have been seeking to reduce consumption by lifestyle changes, typically by reduced heating temperatures, switching devices off, and conserving hot water.

3 in 4 households have been adopting low energy lighting and half of all households have also made other structural changes to reduce energy consumption.

We received a number of specific suggestions, and will be considering them all carefully. Several replies asked the Energy Initiative to "Keep up the good work" in this or other words, and we will seek a way of doing so. Some asked for more specific advice. There is more advice on the energy web pages including copies of the advice printed in the bulletin. We expect to continue to update these pages. They can be reached from www.blewbury.co.uk.

John Richards

Sustainable Blewbury – a new initiative
(Bulletin issue 500)

In recent years the Blewbury Village Society Environment Group has taken several initiatives and actions relating to the Parish Plan and the Blewburton Hill project. The Blewbury Energy Initiative has been the first of a family of new village initiatives relating to sustainable living.

Sustainable Blewbury is prompted by the realisation that in the face of global warming we need to lower our dependency on fossil fuels and to explore ways in which we as a village can adapt to a lower-carbon standard of living, yet maintaining a good quality of life. We are late off the mark and many towns and villages locally and internationally have already started acting on a range of comparable community initiatives.

Sustainable Blewbury has five themes (Energy, Travel, Food, Waste and Recycling and Natural Heritage and Environment). We will be launching the initiative at the Blewbury Festival with a talk by Mark Lynas (author of *Six Degrees*) and also with an Exhibition of all these themes at Blewbury Manor. We wish to involve the whole village and welcome participation from all those with suggestions and ideas on how we can adapt to more sustainable ways of living.

Mike Edmunds and Mike Marshall

MAY

The Cleve BM

Kingfisher on the Cleve JD

drawing RF

Questionnaire Answers

What makes you happy about living in Blewbury?
The kingfishers…..I like living here because my friends are around and there are lots of dogs…..Being able to go to Blewbury School (seven year old)….My wife…..The people, the lack of traffic lights, the streams, and the eagerness of people to get involved…..Access to the Ridgeway…I only have to stick my head out the door and there are people to talk to…..
No street lights (astronomer)...

Does anything make you cross about living in the village?
People's cats…..No, except for dog poo…..One or two of the inhabitants…..The fact that when I arrived in the village there were five pubs. Now only two…. The few vandals about…..There are quite a few toffs with no idea how the other half live and they get my back up sometimes…..The newcomers who don't say hello when you meet them in the village, but behave like tourists and walk by…..Dinosaurs who still light bonfires….. Cars driving too fast: litter: dogs allowed to foul in places where pedestrians need to walk; cars parked thoughtlessly…..People who don't read the Bulletin….No street lights (the same astronomer's wife)...

MAY

drawing RF

THE GARAGE SHOP.
GAYA and BALAN

LOCAL EVENTS

May 27 Lauren James from Blewbury Primary School wins a Karate title in the national championship in the Birmingham indoor arena (*Didcot Herald*).

The results of the Blewbury Energy Initiative survey were announced (previous page).

Sustainable Blewbury initiative announced (previous page).

13th anniversary of the Blewbury Wine Appreciation Society

Roy Wiggins publishes his Short Mat Bowling book

NATIONAL AND INTERNATIONAL EVENTS

May 8 José Carreras announces his retirement from opera singing.

May 12 Several Members of Parliament, including those in high-ranking posts, have been claiming excessive expenses amounting to thousands of pounds.

May 15 British woman of 66 is to become a mother – the oldest known person in Britain to become pregnant.

May 16 Catastrophe in Sri Lanka – 50,000 trapped, 200,000 displaced and 7,000 civilians dead in final offensive of civil war (*Times*).

May 18 Sri Lankan civil war end announced by government.

May 29 Beavers released into the wild in Scotland – the first time they are there after over 400 years.

28

MAY

Sally Jones is a practising photographer and has produced many dramatic images. Here are two of her photographs.

Shakespeare at Blewbury School

Blewbury School is continuing its strong recent track record of putting on Shakespeare's plays with a Key Stage 2 (ages 7-11) performance of a play based on *Macbeth* in December. This production follows hard on the heels of 2008's *Romeo and Juliet* and 2007's *A Midsummer Night's Dream* by those years' Class 3 children (ages 6-7).

As with most subjects, especially those in the arts such as languages and music, early exposure leads to greater familiarity and confidence in later life, and Blewbury School is keen to instil a broad knowledge and enjoyment of Shakespeare in its pupils at an early stage. At a recent workshop conducted in the school, the visiting professional actors were moved to comment on how well the children understood, and how comfortable they seemed with Shakespeare's text.

These could be the Blewbury Players in training, or even the Royal Shakespeare Company actors of the future – watch this space…!

James Wanstall, Chair of Governors

MAY

> **Questionnaire Answers**
>
> **Special Memories**
> Frogspawn in the spring, sledging in the winter, camping in the summer, conkers in the autumn. Catherine Glover's Tea-shop and the Brioche scones….Loads - first time seeing the egg rolling, Christmas Eve every year, the bands playing in the pub this year, when we planted our hedge in the front garden and 47 neighbours called round to see what we were doing and drink tea (I counted - real figure)….Learning to swim in the Mill Pond near the Mill. Deeper then…..Yes plenty. The best was when we all united to kick the Park Owner out of Ladycroft Park…..

Ladycroft Mobile Home Park in 2009 — a happier place than in 2005   - BM

Blewbury Buccaneers

Blewbury Buccaneers began in 2005 as a 'Lads and Dads' informal kick around session on a Saturday morning. Eventually more and more children joined in and in 2007 'Blewbury Buccaneers' was formed with sponsors and a kit and goals donated from Blewbury School. The club has moved on from playing 'friendlies' at U7's to official games in the Oxford Mail Boys' League and competing in various summer tournaments around the local area.

Over the last 4 years the club has enjoyed mixed success on the field - with perhaps our finest moment to date reaching the final of the Hanney U9's tournament. Importantly up to 20 players and their parents and supporters have enjoyed being involved in sport in all weather! All the players who have been involved with the Buccaneers know they are 'Buccaneers' forever and will

remember the experience fondly. Hopefully the team will carry on and football in Blewbury at the school and the adult team will benefit in the years to come.

Bob Brooks, Coach

MAY

The school run - BM

Questionnaire Answers

How do you spend your leisure time?
I play badminton and tennis. I cycle and I appreciate wine!....
I play scrabble and Mah Jong in the winter, and croquet in the Summer, and I belong to the WI....Play Bridge, paint (Art Group), meet with friends.....I run or ride my bike, and if the kids are with me we go to the park..... Digging.....Sitting in someone else's garden.....Helping collate the Bulletin.....Playing pool at the Barley Mow... Painting murals....

Mural in Spring Cottage garden (inspired by Henri Rousseau). Will it be there in 2059?

JUNE

Blewbury Festival (ducks by EL-J)

Festival Programme (EL-J)

Festival Opening at the Family Fun Day (above BM) and tug of war below right PW

Blewbury Festival   JUNE

Boules competition PW

Our Bernard, the official photographer PW

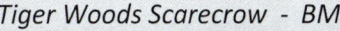

Duck scarecrow

Thief Scarecrow - BM

Tiger Woods Scarecrow - BM

Questionnaire Answers

If you could run any stall in the fête, what would it be?

Fair Trade
Face Painting
China Smashing
Local honey and beeswax products
Hog-Roast

33

JUNE   Blewbury Festival

Glyndebury —Blewbury's Glyndebourne - BM

Tiaras were compulsory at Glyndebury - BM

Charity School — 300 years old - BM

Blewbury Festival   JUNE

Hannah Kidd (Photo Hugo Glendinning)

Downland Dance in Millbrook Cottage garden - BM

Charlotte and Richard Good (professional names Charlotte Brennand and Richard Burkhard) are recent newcomers to the village who are highly skilled musicians and are making a very positive contribution to the village.

Downland Dance in 2009   We gave two performances in Blewbury, the first – in January – being our second Soirée Musicale at the Village Hall. This year we were particularly fortunate in having Adam Harris from Elmhurst School for Dance as guest artist. Living locally, he comes to class with our senior dancers whenever he is here. We were lucky to have the help and support of the Blewbury Players, particularly their light and sound crews.

The second performance was at the Blewbury Festival with an open air show by our youngest dancers in the garden of Millbrook Cottage. With the intriguing title of 'Peter Rabbit loses a carrot' and glorious weather the crowds flocked in to see it.

2009 was a year of outstanding achievements for Downland Dance. Gemma Clegg, in her A-level year at school was invited to dance with Darcey Bussell at the Cheltenham literary festival to launch Miss Bussell's book. Gemma had also danced a Pas de Deux from The Sleeping Beauty with Adam at the Soirée and passed her Advanced Stage 2 exam with Distinction. Adam Harris was given a Dancers' and Actors' Award (a DADA) and Florence Vincent danced several parts in English Youth Ballet's production of The Sleeping Beauty in Swindon.

Lastly, past member Hannah Kidd, now with Richard Alston Dance Company, performed at The Oxford Playhouse, on tour throughout U.K.

In November 2009 excellent results were obtained at the R.A.D. exams – five with Distinction and 30 with Merit.

Anita Rendel

MUSIC FOR A SUMMER'S EVENING

When Richard and I heard that there was to be a Village Festival in 2009 we thought that it would be lovely to take part in a musical offering. St. Michael's is the perfect venue to gather people together and fill the building with song and music for all to enjoy. We compiled a programme that we thought would suit a summer's evening and enlisted the help of some strong burly men to push the piano around the corner on a piano trolley!! We have wheeled our piano to the church on a few occasions and we had an idea that the concert could be used to raise funds for a piano that could stay in the church permanently and be used by everyone.

We are delighted to say that as a result of everyone's support and generosity there is now a lovely Yamaha upright piano in the church. We hope that it will be used by everyone taking part in services and events at the church and contribute to the thriving artistic community of Blewbury.

Charlotte Good

JUNE

Blewbury Festival

An evening with Ron

The village is singularly lucky to have a superb teacher of art and a number of equally superb makers of puddings, and the two combined together to make a perfect summer evening's entertainment. The Women's Institute organised the evening, starting originally with planning for an audience of fifty – what pessimism! They finally had to provide for at least a hundred.

Tony Loy was the host for the evening, and during the interval there was a raffle. Lots of lovely prizes had been given, including bottles of wine, a hair do at the Village hairdressers, a manicure, chocolates and a selection of biscuits. Tony also tried to offer Joyce Gilbert as a prize, but she was not too impressed!

Ron Freeborn has the gift of not only transmitting his own enthusiasm for painting but also the less common ability of showing his audience the subtleties of a picture. In the first half of the evening he talked about the Bruegel painting of the Peasant Wedding. He explained about the horizontal and vertical lines of the picture that define different spaces, how the sloping lines draw your attention to other parts of the painting, the subtle shading and the lovely details of the characters in the picture. What appeared originally to many of the audience quite an interesting picture of life in mediaeval Holland became by the end a fascinating work of genius that can be looked at again and again with a totally different insight.

Of course, Ron's skill is not only as a guide and teacher but also as a painter himself, which he showed in the second half of the programme. By then the audience was replete with scrummy puds, but it's a tribute to the skill of the speaker that nobody nodded off. He painted a market scene, explaining as he worked exactly what he was doing, blocking parts of the market stalls, drawing and painting the people in the market and explaining the reasons for the colour of the background which was not immediately obvious to non-artists. All of that he did with a light touch and a ready wit. He finished the painting later and it was shown at his exhibition later in the Festival.

Karen Brookes and Audrey Long

JUNE

Behind the Scenes at the 2009 Festival

In September 2008, I contacted the Bulletin Editor to see if there were any plans for a Festival to be held in 2009 and he said that he had asked the BVS but they felt it was too soon for anybody to be ready to organise one. This seemed rather a shame as in the past, when the two year gap between festivals widened, it had taken time to establish the pattern again. It also appeared that Festivals had to be held in an 'odd year' as the 'even' years were interspersed with World Cup Football and Olympic Games!

I had been on the 2007 Festival committee but my experience was very limited. However, I took a deep breath and put a notice in the October Bulletin saying that if anybody was interested, perhaps we could explore the idea further. The response was very positive and our first meeting was held on 12th October. It was decided that there was still time to put something together but we would not have an event every day and we would keep it very low budget in view of the current economic state. The emphasis was to be on Blewbury, families and FUN. The invitation was extended to all organisations and groups and the team was growing in number and confidence as we were approached with good ideas and offers to host an event. It was all starting to look very busy.

We had a small core team and co-opted further help where it was needed. Maureen Bale made the most vital suggestion—that it was important to have plenty of tables and chairs, because if people could sit down and were comfortable, they would stay. I oversaw events, following up contacts and ensuring that all was in place for each venue. Sarah Donne and Marilyn Read organised the bar – the most demanding job of the festival: they were taken by surprise on Family Day which was unexpectedly hot and they sold out of every cold drink they had plus the stock for other events.

Sarah and I were joint treasurers, rather vital as we turned over in excess of £12,000. From this, we repaid the £2000 deposit to the BVS and paid out all the expenses for venues, artists, programmes, bar stock etc. We were accountable to the BVS at all stages and teams from the Festival and the BVS met to discuss the fairest way to share out the profit which was just over £5,000.

It was all so encouraging. Ritz de Ridder, who had completed an opera course at the Guildhall School of Music and Drama, suggested inviting a group of opera students to perform and this idea grew into Glyndebury; his wife Elaine said she had always wanted to go to an event where she could wear a tiara – wish granted.

The Blythes at the Manor approached us and asked if we would like to use their new timber framed barn for an event – well, yes, we certainly would and it was the perfect venue for Marianne Suhr's timber framing evening and, also, because of the impressive conservation programme at the Manor, the environment group held their exhibition there.

Music for a summer evening by Charlotte and Richard Good (described on page 35) resulted in the village having a splendid new piano. The WI wanted to hold an event where they could serve delicious puddings and wine, which gave us the *Evening with Ron* - see opposite page.

Then Shanty Group asked if we would like them to put on an evening's entertainment; the environment group invited a well known authority on climate change to speak, Downland Dance performed a ballet, Chris Whatmore gave a talk on plays and theatre in Shakespeare's times. The Boules competition, Bridge Competition, the Curry Lunch, the History Walks, Flower Arranging and Millbrook Walk, the exhibitions weekend, the summer dance, the Fun Quiz, all seemed to fall into place and suddenly we not only had an event each day, but at the weekends we seemed to dash from one event to the next. The open gardens fell into the fortnight and the scarecrows linked it all together.

Saturday 13th June 2009, Family Fun Day which launched the Festival was the most nerve-wracking, but by the end of the afternoon all had gone well, leaving just the four Portaloos in the empty field.

It was quite wonderful and all thanks to the 'many gifts and talents' so generously given by the people of the village.

It was quite sad on Monday 29th June; all the notices and signs had to come down to be stored for next time and the village returned to normal but the community spirit was noticeably stronger and it really was a most marvellous experience.

Pat Mattimore

JUNE

frog EL-J

Blewbury Gardens

On Sunday June 21 six Blewbury Gardens were open for charity in the National Gardens Scheme.

Typical of Blewbury, a few enthusiasts start something and in no time it grows into a whole village event. Today, visitors to Blewbury Open Gardens are guaranteed a great £4-worth for their entry fee. Perfect weather in June is assured, with free parking and picnicking in Hall Barn paddock. Lace-tablecloth teas in a country garden are hosted by Melanie Longhurst, Sue Lay, and Co. (with lawn-side viewing of the Croquet final). Local horticulturalists Lindy Farrell, Sue Russell, Liz Cooper and friends, are soon overwhelmed by the rush to buy their luxuriant, village-grown plants. Well-signposted (thanks to Phil's dad) routes direct folk by sparkling, chalk streams around the village - second chance for more tea and cake at St. Michael's Church - to the open gardens.

The County Organiser reports more phone calls about the opening date of Blewbury Village Gardens, than any other Oxfordshire Garden. So understandable!

Then, of course there are the gardens. Our joining of the 'Open Gardens Scheme' was the brain-child of Rhon Rogers (died 2007), a true plant lover, whose standards we try to maintain. As it said in the 'Yellow Book':

Abners Joyce Gilbert: The view from the gate draws you into this natural cottage Garden. Joyce is President of the Village Produce Association and has stocked many village gardens over the years.

Chapmans Jenny Craig: Informal cottage beds are laid out within gentle, grassy slopes bounded by the Mill Brook.

Green Bushes Phil Rogers: Large range of plants in a variety of settings; ponds and poolside planting, alpine troughs, ferns, pleached limes and roses.

Hall Barn Malcolm and Deirdre Cochrane: Country garden and paddocks with herbaceous borders and kitchen garden, including a quality croquet lawn, C16 dovecote, a thatched cob wall and clear chalk streams.

Nottingham Fee House Carolyn Anderson: Newly planted garden with gravel paths, clipped boxes, perennials and shrubs (photo page 40).

Stocks Norma and Richard Bird: A densely planted collection of lime-tolerant herbaceous perennials offers tiers of colour throughout the year.

This year 730 visitors contributed £5,800 (including £1,000 from the raffle of one of the world-famous sundials donated by David Harber) to support the Hospice system, Macmillan and Marie Curie Nurses, Cancer Research, and other beneficiaries of the NGS charity.

Norma Bird

JUNE

Gardens: This page, clockwise from top left: Abners, Chapmans (Jenny Craig), Hall Barn (RL), Green Bushes (Barbara Baker)

Opposite page: Stocks (RL)

JUNE

Blewbury Festival and open gardens

Garden of Nottingham Fee House (photo Carolyn Anderson)

The Millbrook Walk

The Millbrook Walk has been part of the Blewbury Festival since 1981, when it was started by Simon Rendel. It provides a rare opportunity for visitors, and residents too, to trace the Millbrook from its source in the gardens of Ashbrook House down to Blewbury Manor.

This chalk stream, which joins the Thames just below Wallingford, can normally only be seen in small parts from conventional village paths: the rest lies hidden in gardens. A path involving temporary gateways and bridges is made for one afternoon in each festival, and the route is clearly signposted.

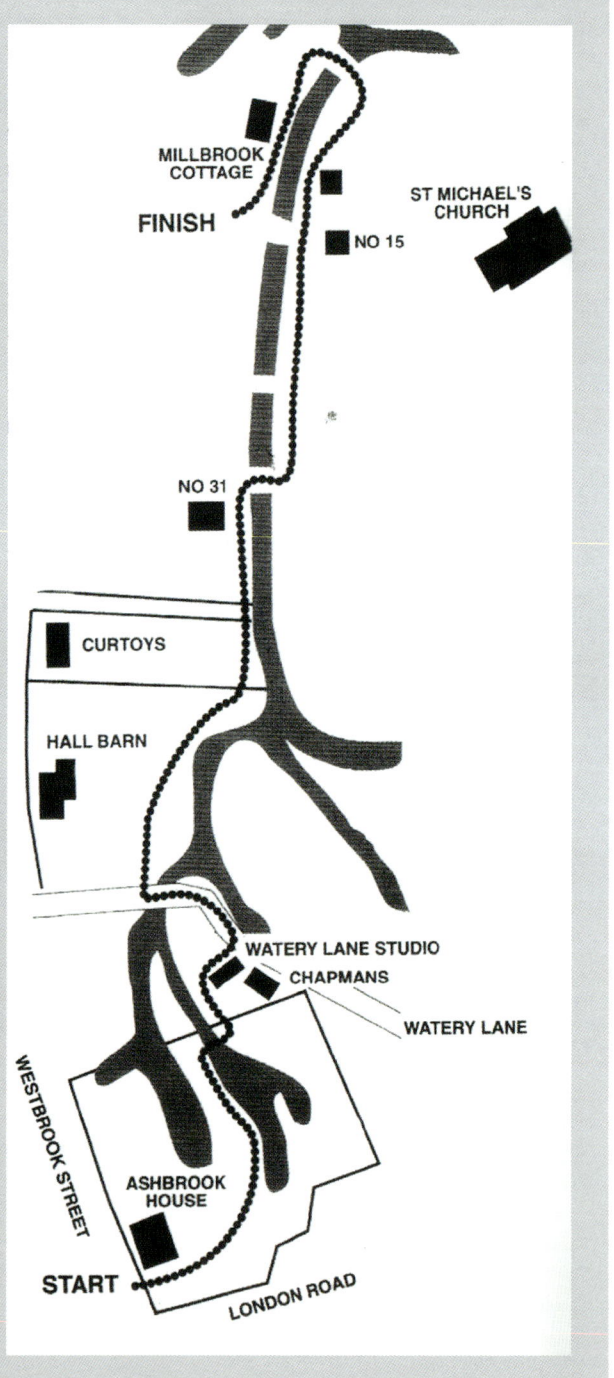

JUNE

Manor gardens - BM

Blewbury Manor - Open Garden

Opening a garden for the National Garden Scheme (NGS) is always a time of excitement and challenges. This year was no exception for us all at Blewbury Manor. More so after being absent the previous year due to two major building projects being carried out - which made it impossible to open to the public. Determined to open in 2009, we had opted for an earlier date of Sunday 14th June for the NGS Open Day to coincide with the peak of the climbing roses and clematis.

Come the day, the gates opened at 2.00pm on a glorious sunny afternoon. First through the door were a couple who had travelled from Northampton! From then on people began to arrive in ever bigger numbers. We could see that we were in for a busy afternoon.

The garden did not disappoint, with much to see and inspire from the clipped box borders of the Parterre, the contemporary Dial Garden, to the more naturalistic Woodland. Wherever there was seating, people sat to admire the views and colours in the borders. And indeed, the roses did take centre stage. The reddish-salmon Albertine, the bold red of Dublin Bay and the salmon pink of Compassion to name but a few.

Everyone took full advantage of teas and cakes being served in the new barn. Phil Rogers frazzled in the heat selling raffle tickets for the Sun Dial which were on sale on our Open Day and also the Village Gardens Open Day. Everyone had a great day and much praise was given to the Head Gardener, Richard Roslyn, who had done such a marvellous job keeping the garden going through all the previous year's disturbances and got it to such a high standard again in time for the Opening.

Nearly five hundred visitors came that day, raising a staggering £2000 for charity in the process. Blewbury Manor Garden had returned with a perfect afternoon.

Jo Blythe

NATIONAL AND INTERNATIONAL EVENTS

June 6 Cabinet reshuffle after Labour does very badly in local elections (*Times*).

June 15 Dissent in Iran about re-election of Mahmoud Ahmadinajad as president (*Times*).

June 22 England's women's cricket team beat New Zealand to win the World Twenty20 final (*Times*).

June 25 Michael Jackson, 'king of pop' dies In Los Angeles.

LOCAL EVENTS

June 7 25th anniversary Garden party for Blewbury Bridge Club.

Francesca Gubbay (née Loy) announced her plan to work as an intern with a law firm representing people waiting on death row in the U.S.A., and asked for sponsors.

JULY

The Thatching of Great Tree Barn.

A spectacular sight on the London road greeted visitors during the late Summer months of 2009. Great Tree Barn was re-thatched; one of the largest thatched roofs in Oxfordshire. The work took about three months to complete often under a relentlessly hot sun and sometimes in rain. Great Tree, now the property of Chris Cambray, was the home of two of the oldest families in Blewbury: the Ilburys and the Humfreys. It is known that Nicholas Ilbury lived here in 1548 and later, by female descent, the family became Humfrey, a branch of the Nottingham Fee Lords of the Manor. The thatchers, brothers Bev and Steve Fowler based in Faringdon, are often to be seen working in Blewbury. Bev and Steve's father and their four sons are all thatchers.

Wherever possible the Fowlers use their own home grown straw to ensure a top quality, long lasting roof. Their land, near Stanford-in-the-Vale, is farmed using the methods and equipment of the 1950's and before. A special hybrid of wheat and rye looking more like barley is grown to give extra length and durability to the straw. Only animal dung is used to fertilise the soil to ensure a low nitrogen input and a weather resistant product. Modern fertilisers use a high proportion of nitrogen to give high crop yields, a matter under close scrutiny with regard to climate change at the present time. Modern harvesting methods cannot be used here; the more gentle and more labour intensive methods of yesteryear have to be applied. The corn is cut and "sheaved" with a 1950's "binder" and then "stooked" in the field by hand ready to be collected, again by muscle power, ready for the "thresher", another machine pre-dating the combined harvesting equipment of the last fifty years. The grain is not of the best grade but can be used for animal feed. In general thatching is a thriving industry at the present time with even new buildings receiving this type of roof. There is also much resistance to replacing old roofs with longer lasting tiles or slates.

Peter Cockrell

The Blewbury Wagon inside Great Tree Barn (Marian Whiting)

JULY

Thatching the barn at Great Tree

Nearly done - BM

Kirsty Bamber thatching - BM

Straw specially grown by the thatchers - BM

Inside the barn - BM

JULY Blewbury's clocks

New traditional clock being built in the Thomson's workshop by Nick Thomson and Dick Street, It will be installed in Lowmans. (right - DS)

Blewbury Church clock (bottom right). The striking mechanism on the right side dates from the early 16th century - RL

Clock workshop - RF

JULY

The Oxford Concerto Orchestra 2009 saw the last performance of the Oxford Concerto Orchestra in St. Michael's Church. Paul Davies MBE and the youth orchestra have performed on the first Tuesday in July since 1980. Many of our local young musicians have been involved. The music has been mainly from the 18th and 19th centuries, but there have also been commissioned works by composers such as Nick Hooper (of Harry Potter fame), Craig Fortnam and others.

Ian Belcher
Ian, like his father before him, is from an old village family and carries on the traditional trade of farrier — nowadays quite often from a mobile forge. *Photo BM*

Blewbury Badminton Club

The Blewbury Badminton Club started the year in fog, driving west to Witney to compete against the Windrush club in the Wallingford and District Mixed Doubles league. The result for Blewbury was as bleak as the weather – a 7-2 defeat. In the following match at home we did much better; we drew the match 4½ all.

This draw and the match we won because the opposition couldn't muster a team were the highlights of the 2008/09 season, which ended with us at the bottom of the league. A change in format for the 2009/2010 season brought better results, fortunately. Badminton in Blewbury in 2009 was not just about the league team.

The club's 24 members gathered every Thursday evening in the Village Hall to play some badminton, chat and have fun. Games were competitive but the banter across the net and from the sidelines was usually more incisive than our shots. Legs were pulled and egos punctured.

On a sunny evening in June, in what was becoming a tradition, the Club gathered on the footpath to Aston Tirrold. They drank Champagne before walking to the Sweet Olive in Aston for the end of season 'do'. The club walked back home across the fields in the moonlight. They had enjoyed themselves. It had been a good season but the following season was going to be even better.

Steve White

JULY

LOCAL EVENTS

July 1 Funeral of Derek Smith, who has written 65 articles for the Blewbury Bulletin over the years. He was extraordinarily knowledgeable about village history. During World War 2 he survived 80 missions with the RAF.

July 2 Liam Roche, who arrived at Blewbury's Churn Stables last November with such high hopes, is quitting Churn because the British Horseracing Authority refused to grant him a licence (*Didcot Herald*).

July 15-18 Production of 'Twelfth Night' by Blewbury Players in the Orchard Dean garden theatre.

NATIONAL AND INTERNATIONAL EVENTS

July 3 Government predicts that by end August there will be 100,000 new cases of swine flu a day.

July 5 Roger Federer from Switzerland wins Wimbledon title making a world record of 15 grand slams.

July 16 Pirates have attacked shipping 240 times in 6 months off the coast of Somalia (*Times*).

July 20 England beat Australian cricketers the first time for 75 years at Lords.

July 25 Harry Patch, the last survivor of the trenches in World War 1, dies aged 111 (*Times*).

July 30 House of Lords ceases to be the highest Court of Justice, being replaced by the Supreme Court.

Nature Notes

Blewbury is a secluded, watery village but it is not proof against invaders: welcome and unwelcome. Most unwelcome are the muntjac deer which strip shoots off our most precious plants. Secondly the harlequin ladybird which destroys our ladybirds. Thirdly the tiny white moth *Cameraria chridella* which is despoiling the leaves of horse chestnut trees in late summer. Lastly one invader that has no legs or wings but travels by water: Japanese knotweed, a pernicious weed which is being contained by constant vigilance. Himalayan balsam has also arrived but is less of a threat.

A recent arrival, the Red Kite, is not an invader; it has been re-introduced to Oxfordshire and is just one of our many welcome visitors. This large, graceful bird is often mobbed by rooks who are unaware that it is not a predator. More dangerous are the sparrow hawks which are resident. Collared doves have found a niche here happily occupying the same habitat as pigeons which are difficult to dislodge so they live side by side. Most welcome in spring are swallows, house martins and swifts but their numbers have sadly declined. We no longer welcome the cuckoo because it has stopped coming.

Other species are disappearing: the honey bee, frogs and toads. Kingfishers still come when there are fish in the streams but the banks where they burrow and build their nests are sadly eroded due to changing water levels and the activity of mallard ducks. Like our water voles they have moved further downstream. Ducks of course survive. Woodpeckers still occupy our trees as do owls, but unfortunately magpies and jackdaws thrive. Many small birds are much reduced in number but the causes are not easy to pinpoint.

Blewbury is famed for its snowdrops together with aconites in the spring. Cowslips are coming back and masses of white violets can be found on hedge banks. For those of us who venture further afield there are wild orchids, wild gentians and helleborines to be discovered. In our Living Churchyard plants which were thought to have vanished have reappeared under an enlightened mowing regime.

Bernardine Shirley-Smith

DEREK SMITH   27.11.1921 – 21.06.2009

It was after reading Derek's articles in the Bulletin that I telephoned him to see if I could call around to ask advice about the book Audrey Long and I were writing on the names of those men on the memorial in the Church. "Of course" said Derek. "I'll just take an hour" I said.

4½ hours later I left Upstones. It was as if I had been in a time machine. Derek held such knowledge of the village and its people.

We talked about football a lot of course. When Derek was a young man sport played a big part in his life. He told me of the football matches he played for Blewbury where the entire team cycled to the away ground, played a tough game in whatever weather, and then cycled home again.

And what of the RAF? – 80 bombing missions with Bomber Command. The chances were really against him surviving - just thirteen missions was the statistical limit. And yet, when he talked about those times as Navigator on a Wellington, then Lancasters and finally Mosquitoes he did so in a matter-of-fact way. One evening we were sharing a rather good malt, talking about flying, and I asked him if he was ever scared? He thought briefly and then said "Well, the first mission I went on when we could only get to 10,000 feet with the unfriendly natives chucking stuff up at us and the Lancasters at 20,000 feet dropping stuff onto us was a bit hairy." The next day he phoned me up "You know you asked me if I was ever scared?" he said, "That Long Wittenham centre back used to frighten me with his tackling." We both laughed.

Derek always took an interest in the village too. What had changed and what the gardens and wildlife were looking like and how things had altered over the years with new people and houses changing the landscape. By being the man he was, and living life the way he did, Derek has left us a wonderful legacy in so many ways. We are so much richer for knowing him.

Mark Palethorpe

In 1999 the Bulletin editors were wondering what to put in the Millennium edition of the newsletter – the first one to be published in the new millennium. To our delight Derek came quietly up to me and asked, in his diffident way, if we would be interested in a series of articles about what village life was like earlier in his life. We jumped at the offer and his first article appeared in the Millennium edition. It was titled *A Village Shop of Bygone Days* (he lived there as a boy) and was typical of the many articles that he has written for the Bulletin over the years – an amazing total of 65 in all.

Derek carried on writing about a great variety of subjects, mostly related to Blewbury and its surroundings and particularly to the people who have lived and worked here for much of their lives, and who have provided the firm base of the local community. His daughter Judith has edited and published most of them in the book *A Blewbury Life*, which includes lots of photographs which were not printed in the original articles.

Another of the things that Derek did for the village, and also for Upton and Aston Upthorpe, which he typically kept quiet about, was his work for the two village charities, the Malthus Trust primarily for children and young people, and the United Charities for older people. He was a trustee of both charities for over 50 years, being Chairman of each for many years. Quietly and effectively he reorganised the funds for the United Charities when he realised that after more than 200 years the funds were not invested to the best advantage. He was the driving force behind modernising the two Almshouses and he was very pleased when he was told "Derek, you will not want for a better memorial in the Village than those two cottages".

Robert Long

JULY

Twelfth Night

Brother and sister were played by brother and sister in the Blewbury Players' production of *Twelfth Night* in the Garden Theatre, Orchard Dene. Alex and Charlotte Cracknell from Didcot played twins Sebastian and Viola in Shakespeare's hilarious comedy of love, mistaken identity and deception. The Didcot Herald reported Alex as saying 'it works because Charlotte can look like a boy rather than because I look like a girl!'

The Players revived the play in their thirty-third season, twenty five years after first performing it. It was directed by Laura Baggaley, an inspirational, young Director who had directed the Players' production of *The Winter's Tale* two years before and had worked as a director at the Regents Park Open Air theatre in London.

A number of new and talented youngsters had turned up for the auditions in April. This placed the romance firmly in the hands of youth (unlike in some previous productions where the romantic leads were well beyond their sell-by dates and required some suspension of belief on the part of the audience) while the comedy was covered by some of Blewbury's more experienced actors. With generous cutting by Laura, this made for a well balanced, fast paced comedy clearly told.

The play was set very roughly in late Victorian times, with bustles, frock coats and top hats and was designed by local artist, Marian Whiting, who created a simple, elegant and flexible set. With an echoing voice transmitted from the Green Room toilet to a trap door in the stage floor, Malvolio's dungeon was cleverly and humorously represented.

In spite of forecasts of a 'barbecue summer', July was horribly wet and a number of the performances were affected by rain. Thursday's had to be abandoned at the interval after torrents of water had all but drowned the famous box tree scene (in which the box tree was played with conviction by the walnut tree growing at upstage centre) and turned the paint on the stage into slime. This got the Players scratching their heads about how to keep up audience numbers in the face of increasingly unpredictable weather conditions. Above all else, they concluded, high standards must be maintained. *Twelfth Night*, which, by general consent, was 'one of the best', would have their supporters coming back for more next year.

Steve White

Questionnaire Answers

Do you work in the village? If so, what are the advantages and disadvantages of working in Blewbury?
Advantage - it's nice and quiet…..Disadvantage - it's quite a way from any major shopping centre for specific supplies.
I work from home - lovely environment but can be a bit lonely.
Advantages: pyjamas, snoozes, pub lunches, dog walks….Disadvantages: nothing outside Blewbury to talk about.
Advantages: my commute is good (healthy for me if I cycle or walk briskly, and good for the environment)….No disadvantages.

Twelfth Night Dress Rehearsal

JULY

49

AUGUST

Village Produce Association Summer Show

The Village Produce Association came about because some villagers during the war decided to pool their resources, knowledge and their excess produce. There are records that go back to shows in the 1940s.

This year the committee took the hard decision that instead of two shows a year, we would hold just one, and maybe vary the time of year sometimes. We decided that Saturday the 1st August, was to be our "big day". We had to change the show schedule quite a lot – not many Sweet Peas or Roses in August, but more tomatoes and courgettes than usual. The committee set up the Village Hall on the Friday evening, putting tables out, putting up the niches for the floral art, marking out the sections and the categories. We had over 350 entries this year, and 39 exhibitors, which was an impressive number compared to the usual, but we were only having one show of course, so all the sections were in one: photography, wine, flowers, vegetables, fruit, children's classes, cookery, handicrafts, and the committee-only section just for fun!

I was awake at 5 am, out in the garden with an early cup of tea and the secateurs, cutting roses in my PJ's, so glad no-one can see me! I had made my lemon drizzle cake the night before – not good, as it went a bit soggy on top (I think it had too much drizzle). I also finished off my flower arrangements, had a shower and hurtled off to the village hall to put my exhibits on the show benches before everyone else came in.

I think the first thing that strikes you on coming into the show, is the scent, totally wonderful, first the floral notes, then an earthy veg smell, and finally, all those cakes and cookery items. Fabulous! The colours of the flowers on display are truly dazzling, and we grew them all between us! The public are always very complimentary about our efforts, even being nice about soggy lemon drizzle cakes. It tasted OK though. After prize giving, in which the coveted Banksian medal went to Eileen Bracken, we packed away, and retired to Maggie and Austin's home in Upton, where we ate the lemon drizzles, quiches and reject cookery items, drank the homemade wine, laughed at the photos, and vowed to do it again next year on the 31st July 2010. Come and join us!

Happy gardening, Karen Brookes

NATIONAL AND INTERNATIONAL EVENTS

Aug 7 Great Train Robber, Ronnie Biggs, freed from prison to a hospital bed on compassionate grounds (*Times*).

Aug 12 Latest UK unemployment figure is 2.4 million.

Aug 23 England won the fifth test match at the Oval to win the overall series 2-1 against Australia and so won back the Ashes.

Aug 24 The Scottish Parliament released Abdelbaset ali al' Megrahi, the man accused of the Lockerbie bombing, on compassionate grounds (prostate cancer). He returned to Libya to a hero's welcome.

Aug 31 Dame Vera Lynn (aged 92) issues album to celebrate 70 years after start of World War 2, and gets into the top 20.

LOCAL EVENTS

Speed limit of 50 m.p.h. proposed for the A417 road from Harwell to Streatley.

Aug 27 The legal battle over Ladycroft Park in 2004-2005, between the then owner and residents (represented primarily by Sheila Austin) was described in the Radio 4 programme *Face the Facts*.

AUGUST

The Barley Mow

Beer at £2 a pint until the first goal...that is a regular offer for a Barley Mow Football Special. Sometimes the drinker wins, but sometimes there is a goal in the first five minutes (which has happened twice and is good for Owen O'Reilly, mine host).

This sets the tone for a pub that goes in for sport of all sorts. It is the place for the stable lads from Woodway, as well as being the setting off point for expeditions to Newbury racecourse and – especially – to Cheltenham on St. Patrick's Day. The oldest lad at Johnson-Houghton's Woodway stables, who still visits the Barley Mow regularly is Bobby Laing, aged 69 and with an official stable lad's number 004 – you can't get much earlier than that. He is said to be the best horseman in Ireland and (they say) came to Blewbury by mistake some 40+ years ago when he had had a little more than he meant to drink on his way from Navan in Eire and went to the wrong stables. When he first came to Blewbury, curiously enough, there was a social division – trainers and owners in the lounge bar and stable lads in the public bar. This no longer holds in 2009.

The Barley Mow is strong on various pub sports. The Aunt Sally Team (leader John Hart) was second in the 2009 Aunt Sally South Oxfordshire league. The Pool A team (Captain Robert Pritchard) won in the Doubles in both the last two seasons, so they are involved in holding some silverware. The B team is a new one and are getting up speed. The Darts Ladies' and Men's teams are getting in lots of practice in their first season.

And the company at the Barley Mow? Well there are Lara, Leo and Harry the dogs for a start. They will always be glad to see you… as will all the human regulars.

Robert Long

photo left - BM - drawing above - RF

AUGUST

Walking bus - RL

Questionnaire Answers

Do you have a favourite view?
Seeing the kids on the walking Bus from Savages to School…..From the A417 near Blewburton Hill…..From Blewburton Hill…..Walks up Westbrook St and looking up to the Downs…..
From the bench near the chalk pit

View over the Chalk Pit - RF

Garden Opera Sunday 23rd August.

This was the ninth annual visit to the garden theatre at Orchard Dene by the Garden Opera Company, this year with Rossini's ever-popular Barber of Seville... the singing of some of the opera stars of the future and the playing of an accomplished chamber orchestra…..picnics on the grass…..a golden summer evening.

Well, it wasn't quite like that, although it had been for most of our previous summer operas – after a summer of bad weather we were lucky not to be rained off, and the audience was wrapped up in rugs and sweaters rather than in summer frocks and shirtsleeves. And still they loved it – not surprisingly since Garden Opera is ever inventive in devising its scaled-down touring productions.

The action was set in Dr Bartolo's Circus, with Rosina The Singing Bird (in a cage, of course) as the star attraction, her disgruntled guardian Dr Bartolo a retired animal-tamer, a wily, personable Figaro, carrying the tools of his trade on his jacket and Basilio an unlikely magician, forever producing scarves, flowers and magic wands from a variety of orifices. Count Almaviva, in one of his many attempts to woo Rosina, was hilarious as Donna Alfonsa, the grey-wigged, substitute singing teacher armed with her knitting and clamouring for a cup of tea and a corned beef sandwich in the updated libretto.

Peter Saunders

Lighting up Blewbury

No, I'm not suggesting we should have street lights in Blewbury – we're not feeble townies. I'm writing this while drinking my reviving cup of tea after having yet again put up (hopefully) romantic red lighting for the Valentine's Dance at the Village Hall.

Do you ever think about the back stage girls (and boys) who make village events sparkle? 2009 started and finished, with New Year's Eve Dance at the village hall. In between, in no particular order, there were two operas (*Noye's Fludde* in St. Michaels and the other one at Orchard Dene), sound for the Red Lion Quiz nights and services on the Play Close, a Festival (lights AND sound for the ballet), the Zombie prom at Halloween, a Comedy Store (we get to play with a follow spot when we do that), and about three weeks setting up for the Shakespeare at Orchard Dene.

But (apart from finding enough orchestra lights) we wouldn't miss any of it. And I haven't got to the highlight of the techie year - Father Christmas on the Play Close! There's getting the lights to work on the sleigh and sorting out Uncle Holly's megaphone, and providing lights so the Brass Band can see to read their music (and

Techies at work - photo Jo Lakeland

they can only do that because the last 3 families living at 27 Grahame Close have allowed us to point our lights out of their attic window)

So do remember us when you are enjoying yourselves at yet another village event – they wouldn't be the same without the techies of Blewbury.

Jo Techie Lakeland

AUGUST

St Michael's Bellringers

Sunday service ringing has been well attended in 2009, as have Friday practice nights, when many of our local ringing friends join us. We are, as always, very grateful for Peter Corderoy's dedication to leading the band in all of our ringing. We have also joined with the East Hagbourne ringers to support St Michael's Aston Tirrold and have rung there on several occasions, including the Christmas Crib service. The photograph shows six members of our band, who won the local striking competition for the fourth time in six years.

Our bells and their fittings are in generally good condition for their age and type, thanks to Dick Street's hard work and regular routine maintenance. We are always looking out for new recruits to train in the art of ringing, and we have recently welcomed one new member, a lapsed ringer of 38 years!

Bishop Stephen Verney was particularly fond of St Michael's bells. For his funeral and in celebration of his life, we rang a quarter peal with the bells 'open' (i.e. not half-muffled as is often the case for funerals) because the Bishop had requested that we make 'as much noise as possible'.

On Wednesday 11th November 2009, we rang a quarter peal half muffled in memory of the fallen:

1260 Grandsire Triples:

Jacqueline Gardner 1, Gillian Loyd 2, Louise Butler 3, Matthew Napper 4, Brian Hunnisett 5, James Blond (Conductor) 6, Richard Loyd 7, Peter Corderoy 8

The ringers again organised the Easter duck race, which raises almost £500 each year for the tower and bell fund – see page 22. Ringing outings are also an important aspect of our year, and in 2009 we organised day and weekend outings to towers in North Oxfordshire, Shropshire and Portsmouth (including ringing at the Cathedral).

Richard and Gillian Loyd

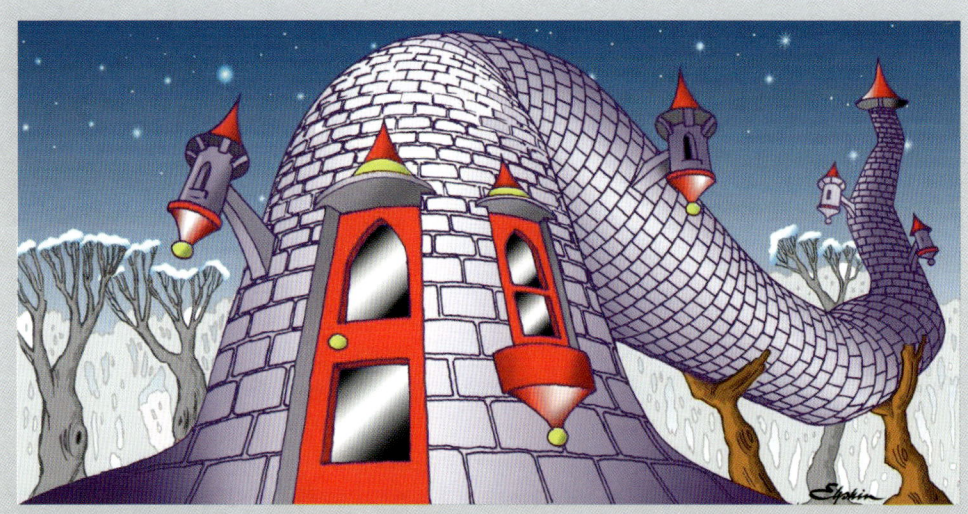

Elphin Lloyd-Jones — the witch's house backdrop for the Wallingford pantomime (see article on theatre opposite)

TV, Film and Theatre 2009

The people of Blewbury, more than most, created their own entertainment. But they also looked to TV, the cinema and other people's theatre to keep them amused.

TV

In September they sat down to watch on ITV1 *Murder is Easy*, an Agatha Christie Miss Marple mystery. Entertaining though the plot was, more attention was paid to the sets, background and continuity, as parts had been filmed in and around St Michael's churchyard the year before.

They also watched the 'soaps', such as *Eastenders, Coronation Street* and *Emmerdale*. These were serialised, neighbourhood dramas featuring strong and colourful characters involved in parallel or intersecting storylines, in many ways resembling life in Blewbury itself. Each episode left viewers guessing what would happen next and provided topics for conversation, speculation and controversy every week in the Red Lion and Barley Mow.

They also tuned in to the unscripted 'Reality TV' shows, such as *How to Look Good Naked* and *Big Brother*, which featured members of the public rather than professional actors, making them cheap to produce. Other shows, such as C*elebrity Big Brother, I'm a Celebrity Get Me Out of Here,* or *Dancing on Ice*, featured minor celebrities trying to revive their careers, who were also cheap to employ. Talent shows, such as *X Factor* and *Britain's Got Talent*, showcased aspiring pop singers and variety acts who, in search of fame and fortune, were subjected to sometimes belittling criticism from the panel of judges.

These programmes were accused of exploiting vulnerable people, of voyeurism and of taking work away from proper actors. However, in Blewbury, as elsewhere, Reality TV was very popular and one of the few genres of television enjoyed together by several generations of the same family.

Theatre

For an off-peak return train ticket of £20 and a seat in the gods for £25 or the stalls for £55, Blewbury residents could travel to London's West End to see a show on corporate greed and corruption (*Enron*), on the state of nation and the demise of rural life (*Jerusalem*) and on existence itself (*Waiting for Godot*), and some did. But musicals dominated, and in December *Legally Blonde* arrived from Broadway. This was adapted from a popular film of the same title and a Blewbury boy, Ed White, was part of the company. Another local lad, George Long, has been in the company for *Sister Act* at the Palladium.

In April, a number of villagers drove to Wallingford to see the Sinodun Players' production of the Ray Cooney farce *Funny Money* at the Corn Exchange. This was directed by former Blewbury resident Erica Harley, who also played Feste in *Twelfth Night*, with posters designed by Blewbury artist Elphin Lloyd-Jones and featuring Blewbury actor Jane Gibson as the police inspector. At the end of the year the same team was preparing for the Sinodun Players' pantomime *Babes in the Magic Wood,* with Elphin designing a set of dominating scale (see below opposite).

In September, the Cornerstone Arts Centre in Didcot celebrated its first year of operation. Many people from Blewbury took advantage of easy access to a wide variety of music, comedy and drama for all ages. The first two shows to sell out in the second season were *An Evening with Pam Ayres*, a very funny, local poet with national appeal, and Sean Lock, a popular stand up comedian.

Cinema

The profile of the arts in Didcot had already been raised when the new five screen cinema opened two years earlier. Instead of travelling to Oxford, Reading or Henley, the people of Blewbury now had the pictures on their doorstep and, in 2009, were watching *Harry Potter and the Half-Blood Prince* or, in newly revived 3D, *Avatar* and *Up*, within twenty minutes of leaving home.

Jane Gibson, Jean Richards and Steve White

SEPTEMBER

Wedding photos on these two pages by mario magé photography

A Blewbury Wedding

Hope Cooper spent most of her childhood in Blewbury and loves the village. When she married Alan Buzza there was only one place for the wedding. Not only did she want to be married here, she wanted to involve as much of the village as possible.

The wedding was held in St Michael's church with the service conducted by the Rev Louise Butler, a Blewbury resident. Other villagers, Ann Croom and Pam Grace, created the floral decorations in the church and the Blewbury bellringers rang the joyful bells as the newly married couple left the church.

Savages, the village's greengrocer and florist, supplied the flowers, bouquets and button holes. Josie Hill, Jeanette Godwin and the full team at Farm Hair Studio worked their magic on the hairstyles and make-up of the bride, bridesmaids and other principal ladies. Sheila Austin and her team at Creative Catering handled the catering for the reception and party, friends in the village helped to make 230 wedding cakes.

The reception was in the garden of Hope's family home at Farthingdown on London Road and in the adjacent garden kindly loaned by good neighbour Gaye O'Nolan for the occasion. This provided a beautiful setting in the heart of the English countryside. An army of friends and family helped to decorate the large marquee and the surrounding garden. Guests were accommodated for the weekend in the Red Lion, Barley Mow, Blewbury B&Bs and friends' houses around the village.

The bridal party walked from Farthingdown through the village to the church and, after the marriage service and a photo session outside the church, Hope and Alan walked back to the reception followed by a long line of family and friends. Walking through footpaths flanked by cob walls, thatched houses and country gardens evoked weddings of earlier times before the age of the motor car.

In place of wedding presents the bride and groom asked for donations to the two charities they support. Hope supports the Children of Sumatra charity which transforms the lives of children in Indonesia by correcting facial disfigurement. Alan supports the Journey of a Lifetime Trust which runs expeditions for disadvantaged and disabled teenagers to transform their perspectives and give them the confidence to change their lives. Wedding donations, with Gift Aid, yielded £4,160 for each of these charities.

On a glorious autumn weekend the sun shone and Blewbury was at its best.

Bob Cooper

SEPTEMBER

SEPTEMBER

Various everyday photos of Blewbury (BM)

SEPTEMBER

The Millennium stone (below) has two time capsules for the year 3000 buried nearby.

SEPTEMBER

More artists than you can shake a stick at

There are two informal art groups who meet regularly. There is an annual trip to Venice, and annual art exhibitions at the school and the church. All mediums are covered, including sculptural and ceramic forms.

1, Marian Whiting - The Downs
2. Ann Edwards - Show-girl-cat
3. Alison Jones - Ceramic Figures
4. Ron Freeborn - Pablo
5. Anne Lawton SBA - Violets
6. Susanne Lay - Boat
7. Elphin Lloyd-Jones - Sculpture
8. Veronica Knight - Venice

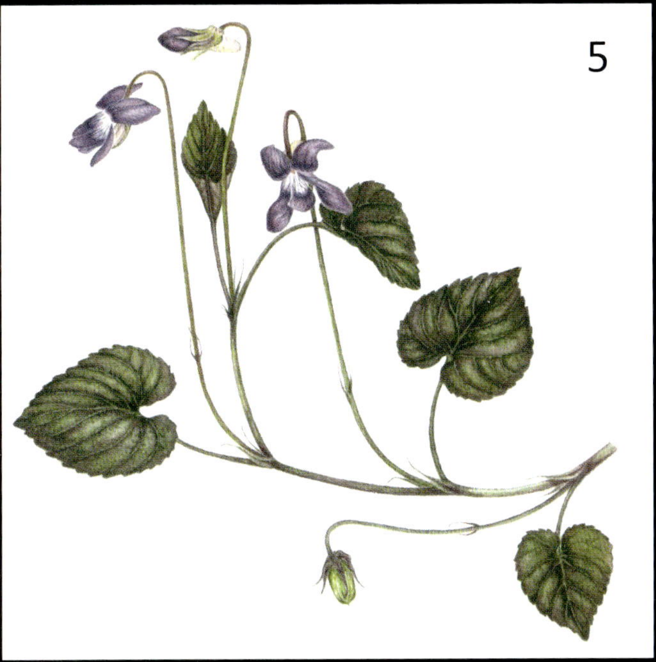

5

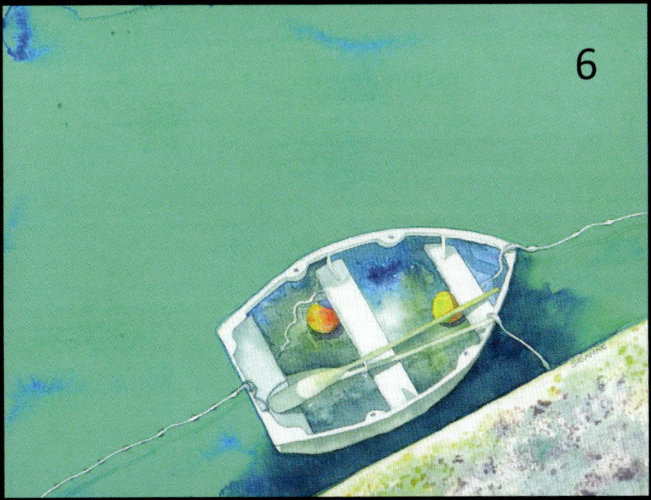

6

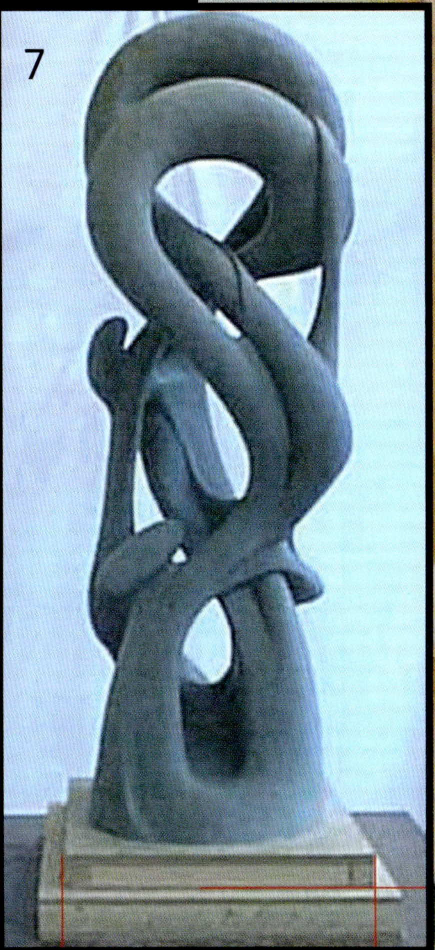

7

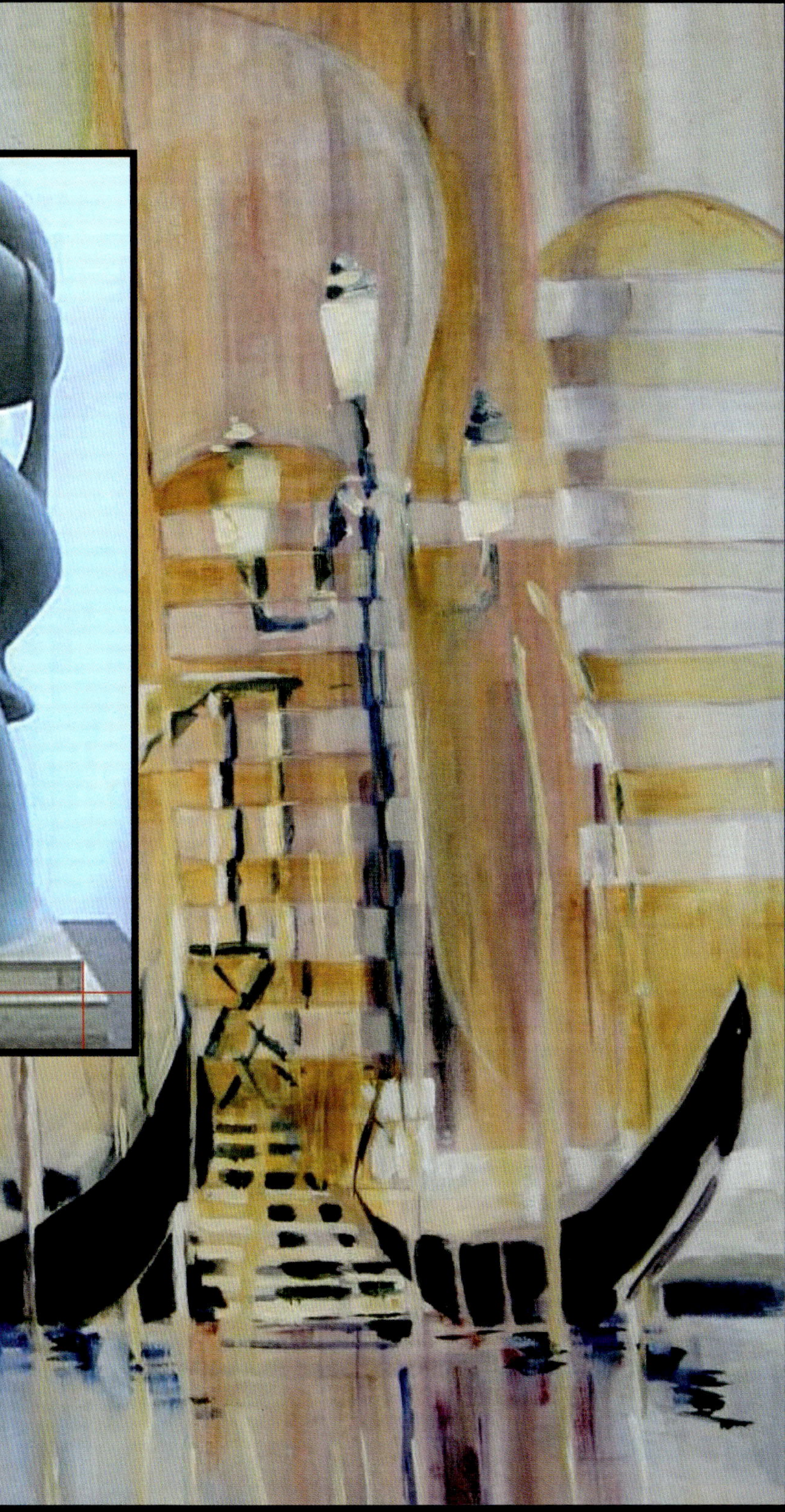

8

SEPTEMBER

NATIONAL AND INTERNATIONAL EVENTS

8 Sep Takeover struggle starts for Cadbury by Kraft Foods of the USA.

Sep 14 Dame Vera Lynn became No. 1 in the UK music charts – at 92 the oldest person to do so.

Sep 14 Melting arctic ice allows two German container ships to sail from South Korea to Rotterdam through the Russian Northeast passage (*Times*).

Sep 28 Hundreds feared dead in freak flood in the Philippines caused by a tropical storm (*Times*).

LOCAL EVENTS

Sep 2 Edna Bonner died – 'Akela' to generations of cub scouts.

Sep 13 'Murder is Easy' broadcast, based on Agatha Christie's story and mostly filmed in Blewbury in 2008.

The 2009 Blewbury Festival made a profit of just over £5,000 for various local projects.

The New Pavilion on the Recreation Ground

The most divisive issue of 2009 in Blewbury concerned a new pavilion for the Recreation Ground. The Parish Council had sold land which had contained the first public tennis court in the village, and there was widespread agreement that the proceeds should encourage the replacement of the existing aged sports pavilion.

The recreational area in Blewbury is on either side of Bohams Road. On the west is the Recreation Ground which contains the old pavilion, a cricket pitch, two football pitches and four modern tennis courts, all served by a small car park. On the east is Tickers Folly field, which was bought, originally by public subscription, to extend the space available for recreation. Tickers Folly now contains a cemetery, a croquet lawn, a half pipe and BMX track, another small car park and a sizeable public area used for one or two public events each year.

There were three main options for the site of the new pavilion. A plan originally developed by representatives from all clubs placed the pavilion next to the tennis courts with a viewing area facing the tennis courts. The hope was that this pavilion would be shared by the tennis, cricket and football clubs. When sometime later this was presented to the tennis club committee for ratification they were not prepared to back the solution. Access to the pavilion would have to go past the tennis courts which they thought would be an unwelcome distraction. The tennis club asked for a small extension of the length of two courts and a larger shelter with a toilet beside the courts.

The most radical option was to build four new tennis courts in Tickers Folly field, and to allocate the space currently occupied by the courts for the pavilion, an extension to the car park, and a court for netball and basketball and five a side football. The objectors to this plan cited the cost of replacing four good tennis courts, the visual impact of tennis courts on Tickers Folly field, and the reduction in the public space on this field.

The Parish Council gave two public presentations seeking feedback on the various options and finally selected the third option - placing the pavilion well away from the tennis courts north of the current pavilion. This is probably the least expensive option but involves switching the main football pitch to face the tennis courts and moving the cricket square. It was strongly opposed by the cricket club. Viewed from the pavilion the evening sun will be behind the cricket pitch. At the close of 2009 the Parish Council had achieved planning permission and grant funding for this scheme.

John Richards

SEPTEMBER

Stepping Stones Orphanage in West Bengal, India

Blewbury has been supporting an orphanage in Dayabari in India since it was started in 2005. The link started when my father sponsored an Indian boy's education. Later, Sanjoy came to England and spent a few days in Blewbury. He returned to his family, got married, and in 2000 I stayed in Dayabri as godmother to his daughter. I started supporting the Stepping Stones educational charity project in the village and, when an orphanage was planned, Blewbury Church and village also became involved. Sanjoy now works for the charity as a trustee.

In late 2008 the orphanage urgently needed money to construct new premises on land they had purchased in Dayabari. People in Blewbury rose magnificently to the challenge and St Michael's Church and its associated Action Group gave valuable support. 2009 has been an exceptional year.

In January Richard Blackford hosted a concert by two outstanding young musicians in Oak Hall House. Many people helped to produce a delicious buffet, and the £1,525 raised was a great boost to the project.

By March the ground floor of the new building was almost habitable. The 400 ft deep well and pump and header tanks were paid for by Blewbury and the children now have pure drinking water. Much of the electrical wiring and a generator was paid for by the 2009 Blewbury Festival. The boys moved in at Easter, a second storey is now planned and an area is being cleared to grow vegetables.

During the year we have sent crayons, letters and drawings from Blewbury children, paid for tables and benches and even bongo drums! Four of the 27 boys are sponsored by Blewbury families.

The team based at the orphanage also does outreach work and has installed wells in two poor villages in the area and supports a maintenance man. Some Blewbury people contributed to cyclone kits which helped desperate people made homeless by severe flooding in the Ganges Delta.

John and I visited Dayabari in early December and were delighted to find it well run with very happy, lively, motivated boys. It was nice to have the Blewbury well pointed out!   *Coral Richards*

OCTOBER

Croquet Club

The fifty or so members of the club enjoyed another happy summer on the lawns.

Play started on Tickers Folly Field in April with a charity one-ball competition ending in a four-way tie. Friendly games, matches and competitions continued through the summer, at both association and golf croquet. The courts were open to all during the Blewbury Village Day on 13 June. Robin Brown narrowly lost in the final of the (British) Men's Championship. Nick Butler and John Spiers were beaten finalists in the British Golf Croquet Open Doubles Championship for the second year in a row, and Nick with Bruce Gallop won the Armada Trophy in Winchester.

September and October saw the winners of the principal club competitions:

> Prebendal Cup: Bruce Gallop
> Founder's Cup: David Spear
> Icknield Cup: David Seed
> Cambray Shield: Malcolm Cochrane

Nick Butler

photo RL

Questionnaire Answers

What one thing would you do to improve the village?
Put more speed signs up and build an older playground (children's comments)…..cycle path to Didcot…..provide more affordable housing for younger people….a lovely path from Sheencroft Cottages to the village…..turn Grahame Close back into an orchard…..drive a tank through the Village Hall…..rebuild the Village Hall.

What do you think of the facilities in Blewbury?
It needs a toy shop (Children's comments)…..Savages selling far more than greengrocer…..a drop-in community centre would be good - not just for the elderly - maybe just a couple of mornings a week…..a café would be great with lovely cakes and decent coffee…..another pub with more settees and decent white wine…..really appreciate Doctor surgery in the Village Hall…..move the National Theatre here….glad I can bank through the Post Office...

When is your favourite time of day?
Sunday morning - seeing people out and about and hearing the bells…..8.45 am - walking home from the school drop-off…..when the kids are in school…..when school finishes (children's comments)…..I feel very peaceful when the night time comes. ….riding my bike through the village I can see the lights in the houses and I imagine what they are doing: cooking, eating, watching TV or just being with each other.

OCTOBER

Local History Group

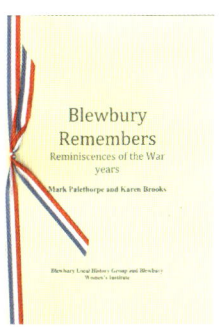

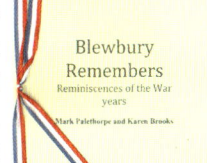

At the end of October the group published a book of memories of World War Two (photo right), recounted to them by a wide variety of Blewbury inhabitants both past and present. Karen Brooks, multi-tasking woman, had collected stories from WI members also and those stories were amalgamated with the history group's collection. Mark Palethorpe, with the help of other members, sorted through the memories and added them to the work he had done on the names of the men on the war memorial.

Wars have some similarities with kaleidoscopes, in which everyone's lives are thrown in the air and land in a completely different pattern. That was very clear with the stories told to the group by so many people. The collecting started in 2007, and in fact is ongoing, but we felt we had to print what we had while there are people around with direct memories of 1939-45. Of course, there are sad events, such as the deaths of the eight men whose names are on the war memorials, but there were also some funny stories. Thanks to the wonders of emails for example we had memories from Australia by Ron Conway, who was an evacuee here during the war and still retains happy memories of schooldays here. Our book will never reach any best-seller lists, but the group feel it's important to record everyday life before it is forgotten. In fact, every meeting is a series of chats about changes in the village and a chance to talk about village characters and events, an opportunity to celebrate quietly the multiplicity of village life.

Audrey Long

WHAT TO DO WITH DAMSONS

Damsons are small plums which grow well in the Blewbury climate and ripen in profusion between August and October. Uncooked damsons are edible but nothing special, but the cooked ones are another story — a brilliant deep red colour and a strong delicious taste (admittedly with quite a bit of sugar). Here are two and a half recipes:

DAMSON GIN   For 800 gm damsons, each damson pricked with a darning needle, allow 1.5 litres gin and 150 gm sugar. Pack the damsons, as soon as pricked, into wide-mouthed jars (jam jars will do). Shake in sugar, pour on the gin. Close very tightly (jam jar screw lids are fine). Invert the jars every 3-4 weeks. Drain off the gin and drink it after 3 months—e.g. at Christmas. Throw the damsons away.

DAMSON JAM   Wash 3 kg damsons, cook gently in 1.6 litres water, stirring from time to time. Remove any stones that rise. Add 1.7 kg sugar, boil briskly continuing to remove stones. Stir continuously to setting point. There will still be some stones, but the taste is very good.

DAMSON ICE CREAM—absolutely delicious. But I can't remember the quantities, so you will have to improvise as you go along. Boil up damsons with enough sugar to sweeten them and use a food processor to turn them into pureé after getting rid of the stones. Freeze it. The day before you want the ice cream unfreeze the pureé, whip a carton of double cream so that it stiffens a little. Stir it in. Taste. If in doubt taste again (remember that frozen food tastes are weaker than before freezing). Freeze again— no special stirring required.

RL

OCTOBER

Top and top right RL

Left and right BM

Solstice Party ("Nibbles with Sybil")

Sybil's home is the small almshouse on the edge of the Churchyard and, for her, that includes the Churchyard too. It's the perfect place for a summer solstice party when most ghosts can be presumed to be sheltering behind their gravestones to avoid the heat and light of our English midsummer.

Earlier in the day Sybil sets out tables and chairs as if she were thirty rather than ninety. All the invited guests bring a plate of food and at least one bottle of wine.

Anyone who passes by is hailed and invited to join us. Some just look shocked at this orgy on holy ground and hurry on by. Most join us, and if it is Friday the bell ringers are press-ganged our way as they leave the bell tower. Our ecclesiastical incumbents have never objected, and this year Jason and Maranda joined us.

If the solstice falls on a Saturday, everything must be cleared away ready for Sunday. One year we didn't manage it and I set my alarm for six to deal with it, only to find my glasses and plates washed up and sitting on my doorstep. Sybil, of course.

However she is not always so sprightly and in June 2009 she was recovering at her daughter's from a fall. So on her 92nd birthday in October Norma Bird cleared out a wheelbarrow and lined it with cushions. In this splendid coach Sybil was wheeled to the Red Lion to celebrate. Volunteers needed for her 93rd!

Sheila Paine.

OCTOBER

Blewbury Garage has a splendid canopy, which is handy on rainy days, but it no longer sells petrol and diesel. The oil companies demand cash payment for thousands of litres when they deliver, which of course the garage only gets back over a long period. It is simply not economically viable.

But the shop is Blewbury's only general store and newsagent, so is very important.

Photo BM

On the garage forecourt is a team of enterprising people from Poland who will wash and valet-clean your car. *Drawing RF*

THE GARAGE CAR WASH

LOCAL EVENTS

Oct 16 Blewbury Bridge Club celebrates its 25th anniversary.

Oct 31 Halloween dance in the village hall.

During October, a speed survey was carried out by Oxfordshire County Council Highways Department on Berry Lane. The average speed was 22 mph and 97% of vehicles were travelling within the 30 mph speed limit.

John Snook retires from mowing Tickers Folly field after many years of voluntary work to help the parish.

OCTOBER

The Benefice Centre (stables originally) for the Churn Benefice, where the Sunday School meets. The benefice covers 7 parishes. Dawn Saunders (main picture) keeps everyone organised. BM

Revd Jason St John Nicolle, Revd Louise Butler and Revd Anthony Lury (BM)

Sunday School

On a sunny day in September about 20 youngsters met at the Brassell's garden barbecue. This was to initiate the launch of the 'Churn Youth Group'. All secondary school children from the benefice of the seven parishes were invited and great fun was had including Dean Saunders and Jordan Cooke with some large Jenga blocks.

Each year Blewbury Sunday School performs a Nativity play on the first Sunday in December. This year an all star cast of youngsters acted out the 'Advent Calendar Puzzle' by Vicki Howie to an enthusiastic congregation including several members of Hagbourne Sunday School and Blewbury Methodist Chapel. The play was narrated by Ellen Bramhill and Penny Brassell and the prayers were read by the Church Music Group. Home-made bookmarks made by Blewbury Sunday School were then given to all members of the congregation and a special 'birthday' cake was then shared.   *Penny Brassell*

Desert Island Discs – 10 October 2009

On this October week Radio 4's Desert Island Discs featured Dame Ellen MacArthur. On 7 February 2005 she broke the world record for the fastest solo circumnavigation of the globe in a sailing boat. Her choice of discs to take on a desert island was

1. Hey Ya by André 3000, performed by Outkast
2. Boys of Summer by Don Henley & Mike Campbell, performed by Don Henley
3. I Wish It Would Rain Down written and performed by Phil Collins
4. Me Gustas Tu — I Like You written and performed by Manu Chao
5. Any Other Name written and performed by Thomas Newman
6. Here with Me by Dido Armstrong, Pascal Gabriel, Paul Statham, performed by Dido
7. Through the Barricades by Gary Kemp, performed by Spandau Ballet
8. Fix You by G. Berryman, J. Buckland, W. Champion, C.F. Martin, performed by Coldplay

The book she would take: SAS Survival Handbook
Her luxury: A fluffy purple worm (which she has taken everywhere).

OCTOBER

Bridge Club

Blewbury Bridge Club has continued to thrive during 2009. It has also been a particularly special year for the club as we have been celebrating the 25th Anniversary of the formation of the club, which was made possible by the completion of the building of the Vale Room in the Village Hall in the early 1980s. This provided suitable facilities for the new club to meet.

Our 2009 celebrations have included a garden party at the Chairman's house, on one of the few warm dry days in early June. It was a great success and enjoyed by all. The second event was again very enjoyable - a dinner held at the Goring and Streatley Golf Club, with one or two fairly informal speeches.

Lastly, we entertained Andrew Robson, the world renowned player, teacher and bridge correspondent for the *Times*, who gave one of his excellent seminars on the subject of Defending Trump Contracts - Observing Dummy. Andrew manages to make his teaching relevant for both experienced and inexperienced players - a truly inspirational teacher.

Over the winter of 2009/2010 another teaching class has been formed for 20 or so new players - the club looks forward to them joining our Thursday night sessions once they are more experienced and to them helping to swell our numbers further. *Mike Allen*

Bridge Lessons

In November 2009 Bob Downey and Roy East, ably assisted by Christopher Smith, took on the challenge of teaching a group of absolute beginners the game of Duplicate Bridge. Each Monday night 20 total novices assemble between 8 and 10pm in the Methodist Chapel for the 12 week course, the aim being to bring participants to a level where they may feel comfortable enough to join and play within Blewbury Bridge Club. Fortified by coffee and biscuits they battle with the mysteries of the ACOL bidding system and desperately try to remember how many trumps are left. It provides a relaxed, informal and extremely enjoyable way to learn this fascinating game — often ending in the Red Lion for a lively discussion on where they went wrong. *Zillah Laidlaw*

drawing - RF

OCTOBER

Blewbury has a long tradition of training race horses — here is one from the Johnson-Houghton stables at Woodway, being trained on one of the many 'gallops' on the downs above the village.
BM

NATIONAL AND INTERNATIONAL EVENTS

Oct 1 60th anniversary of Communist Party rule in China.

Oct 10 Barack Obama wins Nobel Peace Prize.

Oct 15 Study by Cambridge University finds that north polar ice cap will disappear within 20 years (*Times*).

Oct 21 UK population predicted to rise from 61 to 71 million in next 25 years (*Times*).

Oct 22 Postal strike for two days.

Harvest - RL OCTOBER

FARMING IN BLEWBURY IN 2009

We farm 300 acres or 120 hectares of grade 2 land which is mainly arable.

We put 5% of the land in the Stewardship Scheme which provides for wildlife and plant diversity. We have buffer strips along water courses to stop chemical and fertilizer pollution.

The crops grown this year were wheat and oil seed rape. The decision to grow these crops being dictated not by local need but by global demand and price. The price of corn and rape is the same now as it was in the late eighties whilst diesel, chemicals, fertilizer and the cost of machinery and its repair has doubled. The only economy is one of scale so this farm has now been contracted out. The combine harvester typically would cost between £100,000 and £200,000 and the caterpillar and multi till unit, shown in my photograph, cost £200,000.

The Common Agricultural policy still pays subsidies to farmers according to the size of their holding without which it would be difficult to continue. The reason we have no live stock is because they are labour intensive and the paperwork is too time consuming. The main pests are pigeons, dogs and hare coursers who drive their 4x4 vehicles across fields of standing corn.

Chris and Julia Kauntz

Photo Julia Kauntz

John Snook and his tractor on Tickers Folly field - BM

NOVEMBER

Fireworks Night

Unlike the previous year, 2009's bonfire and fireworks night was not subject to rainfall of Biblical proportions and well over 300 people turned out to see a fireworks display containing some of the biggest rockets ever seen in Blewbury.

The BVS spent over £800 on the fireworks this year and the costs of fireworks appears to be constantly rising, along with the insurance, which in these exceedingly safety conscious times, is essential. Accordingly, unlike in other villages/towns where this type of event is often provided for free, a charge of £5 for adults and £2 for children is levied.

Thought continues to be given to this charge, but as it only just covers costs (and for 2009 did not), which includes the baked potatoes provided and which this year were all eaten for the first time in several years, it will probably remain as is for the near term. A more 'fairground' style event could be put on with food stalls and diverse entertainments, which would pay for the privilege and thus cover the costs of the event, but this would be to detract from what is still regarded as a traditional, village 'Bonfire Night' event.

The preparation and tidying up after this event is one of the most involved village events the BVS organises and it would not occur without the hard work of a number of dedicated individuals, from the 'wood collectors' who clearly enjoy riding round the village on tractors, the 'firing team', the 'potato bakers' and the often forgotten 'clearer-uppers'!

Ian Bacon

Building up the bonfire on Tickers Folly Field - PW

LOCAL EVENTS

Nov 7 The annual village Guy Fawkes celebrations were held on Tickers Folly Field, with a large bonfire and a great display of fireworks.

Nov 8 Remembrance Sunday. With the rest of the nation, Blewbury remembered the fallen of Blewbury in past wars with a church service and a ceremony at the War Memorial at the top of Nottingham Fee.

Nov 9 Death of Stephen Verney. All of us in Blewbury who knew him will remember Stephen's friendship and love.

A Tea Room for Savages? Style Acre, a local charity that supports people with learning disabilities, together with Savages, are making a planning application to site a tea room within Savages garden and fruit and vegetable business.

OH SIDNEY!

NOVEMBER

November 14, 2009

Catie Flye and Ian Clarke performed their latest show *Oh Sidney!* in St. Michael's Church. The show honoured the beloved British entertainer Joyce Grenfell and included many of her favourite monologues, sketches and songs. The title of the show reflected one of Joyce's best-known characters – a little boy whose behaviour in his nursery school was clearly too appalling ever to be described in detail. But, although Joyce's humour appeared light and frilly on the surface, underneath there was often a surprisingly darker undertone and this appeared movingly in a telephone conversation, of which of course we only heard one voice, showing the approaching end of a woman's engagement because of her need to minister to her sick and difficult, but clearly much-loved father.

Joyce Grenfell made her first stage appearance in 1939 and went on to tour the world with her performances. Her first solo act was called *Joyce Grenfell Requests the Pleasure* (1954) at the Fortune and St Martin's Theatre, which she eventually took to the USA. She continued to perform her monologues and songs until the late 1960s. She also made countless film and television appearances. This performance of *Oh Sidney!* marked the 30th anniversary of her death in 1979.

Catie, who has directed plays for the Blewbury Players and whose Blewbury cottage is her bolt hole from a busy theatrical life in the United States, has, with her musical cousin Ian Clarke, given performances based on Joyce Grenfell and Ivor Novello throughout the UK.

Peter Saunders

Stephen Verney - photo Derek Wagon

Stephen Verney - *from the Blewbury Bulletin, December 2009*

Stephen came to Blewbury in 1982, when he and his wife, Sandra, bought the Charity School House. They had fallen in love with the village, and with the house, which they called "Harry's gift". Harry was their infant son; he was born and he died while they were completing the move to Blewbury.

Retirement as Bishop in 1985 led to his moving permanently to Blewbury, and joyfully taking part in many aspects of village life: making music – he sang in the opera, started a male voice choir; gardening – his love and skill with this enabled him to create a beautiful and interesting plot; going to the village church.

The island of Crete was a place which he particularly loved, because during the war he spent time working there as a secret agent. MI6 had recruited him because they thought that reading Greek at Oxford would be useful!

Stephen always found time for people: to listen to them, to give advice, and above all to make them feel good. All of us in Blewbury who knew him have been enriched through Stephen's friendship and love.

Janet Wagon and Mike Edmunds

NOVEMBER

Mary Ritchie

Mary, who died in November 2009, ran the Borlase Gallery for over 30 years. She was very involved in village activities and was a real inspiration to local artists and the cultural scene. The stylized painting of the gallery is by Roy East.

From the Blewbury Bulletin, Christmas 2009

Mary and John's contribution to Blewbury cannot be overstated. From their arrival at Borlase in the early 1960s they both entered wholeheartedly into village events.

Borlase Gallery became a cultural centre and Mary ran the Box Office for Peter Sheldon's pageants, Music Halls, Operas, Blewbury Festivals and many Blewbury Players productions. Many artists owe a real debt of gratitude to Mary for her promotion of their work. She was herself an enthusiastic artist and a regular member of the annual Venice painting course. Borlase was also the focus of much music-making in Blewbury and after John died, Mary donated his Bechstein piano to the Village Hall.

During the past few years, despite memory loss, she was always smilingly ready to welcome her many friends for tea, biscuits and a long chat. Mary's great charm and personality will always be in our memories.

Ron Freeborn and Peter Saunders

NOVEMBER

2009 for me

Our Beloved Majesty celebrated her 'annus horribilis' a while ago — mine was 2009 with some leftover bits from 2008. Having come to Blewbury in the mid-1960s and built Morters as our family home, I was eventually left there high and dry on my own, happy to stay until removed in a coffin. However, a series of blackouts, crashes and falls from the top of high-gabled Dutch houses put the kybosh on that idea. Obliged to quit Morters at the height of a property slump, I accepted the kids' idea of renting it out. Fine, except that I had to move out quickly.

When we first came here, there was Paddy the tramp, who frequently fell in the streams, looking for somewhere to bed down on leaving the Red Lion, but since then everyone had a roof over their head. Where to go?

The first house offered to me was Farnley Tyas — a beautiful old house, but with a staircase that required a gold in downhill slalom to negotiate. After that a royal bedchamber at The Cleve with a high four-poster bed and a mounting stool. Then wandering exile — Kettering, France, Westbrook Green, Brighton, Paris, Isle of Wight, Cyprus — until I could move into Little Morters, a cobbled-together patchwork of a house which is sweet and has the overriding merit of being in Blewbury.

Buses to Didcot pass every hour and once you get to Didcot station, the world's at your feet — Samarkand, Timbuktu. Reading even. So my horizons remain wide. Just the closer ones are closing in. Wallingford is still just about OK – the weekly market-day bus a friendly meeting-place for old ladies with shopping trolleys – but Sibford Gower (where my car came to grief) now lies on another planet. Even Dorchester proves difficult.

It's perhaps best to take refuge in the thought 'why would anyone want to leave Blewbury anyway?' – Savages have everything, the garage everything else and the Post Office all the other everything elses. Even high culture is catered for, from opera to the Boxing Day walk.

2009 was also the year my professional career came to a star-spangled end as the visiting international celebrity at a textile symposium in Vancouver — where I ate Canadian smoked salmon with Mary and Erwin Seibold whom I normally drink vodka with at The Old Malthouse. It also marked the celebration of my 80th birthday with a party at Cochrane's barn, surrounded by old friends from elsewhere and dear Blewbury faces. I'm staying here.

Sheila Paine

Questionnaire Answers

More Special Memories

Playing on Blewburton Hill and collecting walnuts (children's comments)…..Too many to mention - but during the festival this year when there was an exhibition at The School House and a Pig Roast outside. It was reminiscent of all such sunny summer days from the past when families came together and celebrated life in Blewbury…..Dressing up as a Dalmatian alongside 100 others on Boxing Day….Walking along the Millbrook Walk—which links many back gardens that are next to the mill stream and is only open once at each festival…..My next door neighbour on being introduced to my baby son saying "carrot bonce!"…..
I haven't left yet.

Piece of music or song

Oklahoma...Bohemian Rhapsody (Boxing Day in the Red Lion)...Lark Rise by The Albion Band (particularly the mowing song)...Christmas Carols...The Snow Queen...Blueberry Hill…..

The music hall song "I Live In Trafalgar Square". It reminds me of the early Music Hall shows held in the village……

The Coventry Carol as it was used in *Sir Gawain and the Green Knight* - the first Opera that Blewbury commissioned…..

I found my thrill on Blueberry Hill….

NOVEMBER   Blewbury School

2009 was very fresh and the teachers had only just remembered not to write 2008 on the board when the inspectors descended. An OFSTED report that remarked that the school was "good with outstanding features" meant that the village school was doing what we already knew - a great job!

With nearly one hundred and fifty children descending on the school each day it is the focal point of the village for an hour in the morning and again in the afternoon. Once all children have disappeared inside and mothers, grandparents and a few fathers have departed, it is difficult to believe all that goes on behind the front door.

Early morning clubs in 2009 include, amongst other things, karate, multi sports and ICT. An eight year old black belt is a terrifying proposition yet she sits in class 5 working on her literacy skills with all the others.

Blewbury School as always took education far beyond the classroom during 2009. The number and diversity of the trips and visits were vast. The four year olds were walked through the village to see Mrs Barton's chickens and understand where eggs really come from. Students at the other end of the school visited Sweden to forge links as part of the Comenius project. For many within the school it was residential trips to Cheddar, Kilvrough and more locally to the Ridgeway Educational Centre, where they were forced to turn off their Nintendos and watch the red kites. Blewbury School also welcomed visitors, including two teachers from Uganda. This visit may have brought home how small the planet is and to some extent how vulnerable it is at the moment. To learn about sustainability is vital and Blewbury Primary, as always, approached this in a practical fashion in 2009 with hoes and spades digging a plot for the vegetable garden.

Throughout the year the children performed - singing, dancing, acting and playing instruments. From the *Romeo and Juliet* of the 6+ year olds to the Gangsters and Molls in *Bugsy Malone*, not one over the age of 11. And the circus day brought a whole new set of skills and more excitement for the children as well as health and safety nightmares for Mrs Mills.

The year started to wind down with more Shakespeare in the form of *Macbeth*. The dagger-wielding 9+ year old egged on by his similar aged Lady. After which a more traditional run up to Christmas with the Carol concert sung in an Oxford square, and finally the Nativity where the youngest members of the school adjusted their halos and waved at their parents.

2009 was the tercentenary of the school, and like the rest, full of everything that a school should be. Work, play and laughter, all the ingredients needed for the future of Blewbury.

Tom Laugharne

NOVEMBER

Opposite - lunch - BM. Above - Blewbury school field - BM

Busy in school - BM

Flying Squad

The Blewbury Flying Squad was founded in 1983 and is a car scheme provided by volunteer drivers using their own cars to transport Blewbury residents to doctors' surgeries and local hospitals, including dentists, opticians and chiropodists. The service is funded by voluntary donations from users of the service. In 2009 we geared ourselves up for a potential flu epidemic which never happened. In the event, 2009 was a quieter year than normal with 50 trips recorded compared to 160 trips in the previous year. The Flying Squad had 22 drivers available during the year.

Ian Parsons

NATIONAL AND INTERNATIONAL EVENTS

Nov 3 Five British military personnel were shot dead in Helmand province by a "rogue" Afghan policeman, bringing the total British dead this year in Afghanistan to 92 and 229 since the start of the conflict in October 2001.

Nov 13 First woman pilot in Red Arrows (Times).

Nov 19 Serious floods in Cumbria. Record rainfall – 314mm in 24 hours – in Borrowdale (Times).

Nov 20 Large Hadron Collider in Geneva achieves its first particle collision. Several people in the local district have been involved with this massive international project.

Nov 24 First public hearing of the Chilcot Inquiry into the Iraq War.

DECEMBER

Red Lion - BM

Photo BM

LOCAL EVENTS

Dec 11 Mrs Ruby Weeks had her 100th birthday - a lively happy centenarian.

Dec 21 Snow fell heavily during the afternoon in Blewbury and surrounding villages and towns. Traffic in Reading was grid-locked. But St Michael's Church was full to capacity for the annual Blewbury Carol Concert.

Dec 24 Christmas Eve ,   Dec 26 Boxing Day, Dec 31 New Year's Eve - see later pages

Questionnaire Answers

What advice would you give to anyone moving in?
Read the Bulletin…..Send your children to the village school and they will always have a sense of belonging…..Don't bring a cat….. Don't light a fire in the middle of the village (Children's comments) …..Get involved…..Don't be standoffish...

How do you spend Christmas and Easter?
Digging…..Christmas is always in Blewbury - Christmas crib service - Father Christmas - Drink - Wake-up presents - Pub….. Fishing plastic ducks out of the stream during the Duck Race…..Lighting tea lights in Church ready for midnight mass….. Boiling and decorating my egg for the Egg-rolling…..Chipping sheet ice off the Church path on Christmas Eve

Sum Blewbury up in one word.
Idyllic/Peace/Endangered/Welcome/Home/Brilliant!!!/Delightful/ Community/Affluent/Fortunate/Involved/Unique/Friendly

DECEMBER

RELOCATION, RELOCATION

We located and purchased a house in Blewbury in 2005, which proved to be a most memorable year for us. We had previously lived and worked for most of our lives in the glorious West Country which boasts enchanting villages and spectacular scenery and coastline, so the move to the centre of England was not to be made without some trepidation! After all, we would be no longer able to take a drive to the Dorset coast for lunch and be home in time for tea!

We arrived to view the house in Bessels Lea in mid-June on a perfect summer day. Being somewhat anxious to see what we might be letting ourselves in for, we arrived at least an hour ahead of the appointed time to explore the location - our route taking us along South Street and into Watts Lane. That walk will always remain memorable. Firstly the imposing thatched Orchard Dene met our eyes, together with the then owner's large golden retriever (Harris) hesitantly wagging his voluptuous tail! We followed along to the edge of the stream where we had a totally unexpected sight of literally hundreds of miniscule frogs crossing from the stream into the adjoining ditch! It was difficult to avoid stepping on the small creatures! The warm weather was obviously inspiring them to relocate also... .incidentally, since that day we have never seen another frog in that location! Our walk followed on through the beautiful churchyard, past the ancient Church and then back to Bessels Lea. Pausing outside the house we said (somewhat rashly!) "It doesn't matter what the house is like inside, we will buy it!"

Blewbury is a village of long tradition and sense of pride in its long history. It is noticeable that people join the community and seem to stay forever. I frequently ask "how long have you lived here?" At first I was surprised and impressed when the reply was 30 plus or 40 plus years! Now I understand...

An outstanding feature of Blewbury is the number of and varied community activities available - any of which make you welcome. Our own interests include the Local History Group, which provides a source of great knowledge and interest, ranging from listening to past anecdotes to, most recently, looking for lost tombstones in the Churchyard! The variety of flora and fauna is impressive, from the shy Muntjac to the soaring majestic Red Kite which regularly circles local gardens. Never before have I seen or heard such a profusion of Skylarks as I did the first time I explored Blewburton Hill.

Maureen Bale

I guess in a word Blewbury is "verdant". So say many of the visitors that arrive here for various meetings. As they trip over the bridge to our front door, and pause a bit, disturbed by the splash of the fish below, many look around and say the village is at peace with the rest of the world. In my spare time I do voluntary work as County Adult Training Manager for Oxfordshire Scouting, and this role means I regularly see pretty much all of the County but never tire or regret living in Blewbury even though it's more or less at the southern tip of the known universe.

Tradition at Christmas tends to be thrown to the four winds as we decide to dispense with the usual meals and choose one of our all time favourites, such as steak and kidney pudding (very healthy) or simply egg and chips! What's important to us is simply enjoying the time together and what better place than Blewbury.

Patrick Farr

DECEMBER

Christmas Eve

By tradition, Father Christmas sets off around the village on Christmas Eve, hauled by some sturdy reindeer disguised as humans. They end up in the Play Close where presents are distributed to the children.

At the same time, the Band play carols which those present join in singing lustily.

On this page
Below: The reindeers and FC assemble - PW
Right: Arriving at the Play Close - BM
Bottom right: Uncle Holly - Chris Willison

DECEMBER

On this page (all BM) -
Top and bottom left: The Band
Top right: Giving out the presents
Bottom right: Father Christmas and team

DECEMBER

The Boxing Day Walk

The new route for the Walk in 2009 (drawn by EL-J). Points 1, 2, 3 and 4 are where the walkers stop for beer or soft drinks

The end of the walk at the Playclose. BM

Questionnaire Answers

Any other thoughts?

It is a very warm and friendly village to live in if you choose to let it be. It is one of the most active villages I know. Many people give a lot of time to make it the place it is….. At present there is a deep community spirit here, hard to pin down but active and highly effective nevertheless. The number of thriving and evolving clubs and societies testifies to this, as do the many people willing to devote large amounts of their time and energy to the preservation, improvement and celebration of village life and this precious environment…..

We love the church bells, the lack of street lighting - and the range of talent in the village….. We need an influx of young people with fresh new ideas and enthusiasm….. We need affordable housing to keep young people in the village.

The Boxing Day Walk

DECEMBER

BOXING DAY At 10.20am, with the parade due to start in ten minutes, the Chair of the Village Society was seen to be in a slight state of concern. "Where is everyone?" he remarked to the Walk Leader, "Has the change of route ruined the whole thing?" As it turned out, he needn't have worried, as a late rush of entries saw a total of 78 adults and 36 children taking part.

2009 saw the 40th anniversary of the walk and a delve into its history revealed that it had taken on a number of guises and formats over the years. With this in mind and the increasing difficulty of stewarding the London Road (which is no fun for anyone over the Christmas period) it was felt a new route would be trialled, one that brought in other parts of the village, reflected the fact we are down to two pubs and reduced exposure to the potential perils of the one-off idiot driving down the London Road.

So, with this new route, off the intrepid walkers set at 11.00am, having paraded and performed their skits in the Village Hall car park, finishing off at the Play Close, after what turned out to be an overlong, but still enjoyable route via Westbrook Green, Bridus Mead, The Barley Mow and the Red Lion.

Highlights included the BMP (Bridus Mead Party) attempting to assert the independence of their corner of the village against this new proposed annual invasion, a troupe of Canadian Mounties singing songs and various takes on the BBC's Strictly Come Dancing and political events of the day.....oh, and some chap called Ron Freeborn as himself....but some might dispute this being called a highlight....

As with the 'Bonfire Night' a few give a lot of their time to put on this perennial village favourite, taking them away from their families at the festive time of year and this is easily forgotten. However, such is the joy of this event, here's hoping there will always be people in this village prepared to make this effort.

Ian Bacon

The walk past the Cleve - PW

DECEMBER

NEW YEAR'S EVE

Oh what a night! - to quote a song, but it really was a fantastic evening in Blewbury to mark the end of a decade.

I was on the stage singing away and watching everyone - young and old - boogying on down to the music that we had been rehearsing for months. The Richards were first on the dance floor and last off, and were joined by so many Blewbury folk dressed in the black, red and white colours. I loved every minute of it and could have carried on until the morning - well it was 12.45 by the time we had finished which was probably late enough anyway!

The village hall looked transformed, festooned in black, red and white posters, parachutes and the disco ball (thanks Alex again!) And wow, the ladies toilets, I just had to spend longer in there than normal - it looked positively posh!

At midnight we stopped playing and put the radio signal on to pick up the Big Ben count down for New Year. It was wonderful to be sharing this time with so many friends and gave me a real warm feeling of pure happiness.

Dysfunktional have played quite a few gigs now, but none match the buzz and the good will that comes from playing in the village hall to the Blewbury crowd.

Janet Morgan

A joint sub-committee formed from the school Governors and members of the PTA organised the event as a fundraiser. We didn't want people to have to make a special effort with a particular costume theme, as is usually the case with Village Hall parties, so we came up with the idea of red, white and black, enabling everyone to dress up or down as they wished. The colours were echoed in the decorations, which included red helium balloons on black and white tablecloths, as well as a giant parachute, a glitter ball and lots of fabric. I'd spent hours trying to transform the Vale Room, a highly useful and practical room exuding all the ambience of a morgue, with hundreds of fairy lights, only to be told by a governor that it looked like a tart's boudoir.

This was an excellent time to stock up for the bar as the local supermarkets (Sainsbury's/Tesco's/Waitrose) were involved in a price war on alcohol. We were able to buy at very competitive prices and subsequently made a profit of just under £900. Deciding what to buy was tricky. We knew that in the past people had brought their own refreshments to New Year's Eve parties in the Village Hall, and we had to have a range of drinks which would attract the widest possible market.

Tickets were selling very slowly right up until the big night. At one meeting two weeks beforehand, the committee were debating how many tickets we had to sell just to break even. Then, during the week between Christmas and New Year (probably for many the pressure was off and people could start to think about life after Christmas Day), there was a sudden rush at the two outlets, Savages and the Post Office. We sold 192 tickets.

The atmosphere was fantastic. When I wasn't dancing or manning the door I was helping to clear empties from the tables. There were a lot of empties, but the image I'll remember is the smiling. Everyone was smiling, all night. Whether it had anything to do with the huge consumption of alcohol (we had trouble getting rid of the bottles, and some of us had to store some in our green boxes which were already full from Christmas), the brilliant sounds from the band, or a combination of both, the organisers felt very proud of ourselves. We made over £2300 for the school.

Jo Laugharne

DECEMBER

The last day of 2009

2009 → 2010
@ Blewbury Village Hall
Dress = Anything Black, White or Red

Happy New Year

Doors open 8pm
Tickets £12
from Post Office & Savages

Fundraising Bar
Profits to Blewbury School

Live Music From Blewbury Band "Disfunktional"

NATIONAL AND INTERNATIONAL EVENTS

Dec 10 Sarah Palin, who was Republican vice-presidential candidate in 2008 and might be a presidential contender in 2012, claims that global warming is a hoax (*Times*).

Dec 18 Copenhagen climate conference finishes, but the deal announced falls far short of the minimum target the IPCC (International Panel for Climate Change) has recommended (*Times*).

Dec 30 Umar Farouk Abdulmutallah, a Nigerian student who had studied at University College, London, tried but failed to blow up a transatlantic airliner bound for Detroit on 26 December with explosives in his underpants.

NEW YEAR'S EVE BAR PRICES

Red Wine
  Hardys Bin 53 Shiraz   £10.00
  McGuigan Bin Series Merlot   £10.00

White Wine & Champagne
  First Cape Chardonnay   £10.00
  Sainsburys Cava   £12.00
  Etienne Dumont Brut Champagne   £20.00

Beers & Lagers
  Old Speckled Hen (bottle)   £ 2.50
  Stella Artois (bottle)   £ 2.00
  Carlsberg (can)   £ 2.00

Bulmers (bottle)   £ 2.50

Smirnoff Ice (bottle)   £ 2.00

Soft drinks (can)   £ 1.00
Water (1.5ltr bottle)   £ 2.00

Satellite photograph of Blewbury in 2009 (© Google 2010)

In 1967 we produced a publication 'Blewbury – A Self Portrait'. It was exactly that – a reflection of the village at that time. 'Blewbury 2009' is similar but relates to a specific year and incorporates national and international events, and says something to future generations about our lifestyle and interests. The two main influences have been Flora Thompson's 'Lark Rise to Candleford' and the Penguin Anthology of 'Picture Post', quite diverse publications but very important source material for period film and TV programmes. I would like to think that in 2059 some young director/writer might refer to this book in making some minor epic.

Ron Freeborn